Thinking and Reasoning: A Very Short Introduction

VERY SHORT INTRODUCTIONS are for anyone wanting a stimulating and accessible way into a new subject. They are written by experts, and have been translated into more than 45 different languages.

The series began in 1995, and now covers a wide variety of topics in every discipline. The VSI library now contains over 500 volumes—a Very Short Introduction to everything from Psychology and Philosophy of Science to American History and Relativity—and continues to grow in every subject area.

Very Short Introductions available now:

WORK Stephen Fineman
WORLD MUSIC Philip Bohlman
THE WORLD TRADE
    ORGANIZATION Amrita Narlikar

WORLD WAR II Gerhard L. Weinberg
WRITING AND SCRIPT
    Andrew Robinson
ZIONISM Michael Stanislawski

## Available soon:

For more information visit our website

www.oup.com/vsi/

Jonathan St B. T. Evans

# THINKING AND REASONING

## A Very Short Introduction

# OXFORD

UNIVERSITY PRESS

Great Clarendon Street, Oxford, OX2 6DP,
United Kingdom

Oxford University Press is a department of the University of Oxford.
It furthers the University's objective of excellence in research, scholarship,
and education by publishing worldwide. Oxford is a registered trade mark of
Oxford University Press in the UK and in certain other countries

© Jonathan St B. T. Evans 2017

The moral rights of the author have been asserted

First edition published in 2017

Impression: 6

Published in the United States of America by Oxford University Press
198 Madison Avenue, New York, NY 10016, United States of America

British Library Cataloguing in Publication Data

Data available

Library of Congress Control Number: 2017936443

ISBN 978-0-19-878725-9

Printed in Great Britain by
Ashford Colour Press Ltd, Gosport, Hampshire

# Contents

# Acknowledgements

I have researched and written on the topic of thinking and reasoning my entire adult life, since I started my PhD studies in 1969. I had the enormous good fortune to be supervised by Peter Wason, the father of the modern psychology of reasoning. Without Wason's inspiration and mentorship my life would have been very different and this book would never have been written.

My studies of this topic benefitted from collaboration with a number of talented researchers along the way, all of whom helped to shape my thinking about thinking. In particular, I should mention Steve Newstead, Simon Handley, David Over, and Valerie Thompson. I would also like to acknowledge the influence of Phil Johnson-Laird and Keith Stanovich. While I have collaborated formally with each only once, our frequent exchanges of ideas have challenged and inspired me over many years.

Finally, I should acknowledge some direct help with the writing of this book. Linden Ball filled some gaps in my knowledge and both Shira Elqayam and Jane Evans read and criticized the entire draft. I am grateful to them all.

# List of illustrations

# Chapter 1
# Introduction and history

The French philosopher Descartes famously said 'I think therefore I am'. Thinking is indeed the essence of what it means to be human and defines us more than anything else as a species. The remarkable success of humans, far ahead of all other animals, is based on our unique powers of thought. By thinking, and especially by reasoning to a purpose, we can exercise all the formidable powers of human intelligence. Reasoning can help us to solve novel problems, to make one-off decisions, to develop mathematics, science, and engineering, to design our environments to suit ourselves. We can even use thinking to study thought itself, as philosophers and more recently psychologists have been doing for centuries.

The capacity for human reasoning is extraordinary. Reasoning involves making suppositions and inferring their consequences. This may be complicated—involving mathematics, for example. But what makes great thinking so difficult is having the imagination to ask the right questions, or the ability to see things from a completely new perspective. When Einstein developed his theory of relativity, the physics of Isaac Newton was so strongly supported by available evidence that there seemed no reason to question it. Almost all known experiments confirmed his predictions, but there were some odd studies suggesting that the speed of light did not depend on the speed of the source from which it was emitted. In trying to understand this, Einstein somehow came up with the idea that the speed of light was constant, which meant that time had to be relative. All previous physicists, including Newton, had assumed time to be absolute. From this immensely creative idea, with the help of a great deal of complex mathematics, came the theories of special and general relativity that revolutionized physics.

One of my favourite examples of the power of human reasoning is the breaking of the Enigma code by Alan Turing and other mathematicians secretly assembled at Bletchley Park, England, during World War II. Enigma was one of the most important cyphers used by the German Command to encrypt secret communications broadcast by radio. The Enigma machine was a complex and clever invention with a keyboard connected to several rotors that could be set up in many combinations. It also had a plugboard with adjustable cross-wiring to greatly increase again the number of starting positions. With every keystroke the rotors turned, changing the encryption code for each successive letter typed in. Yet, by the time the first Enigma machine was captured, the Bletchley mathematicians already knew what it looked like, having deduced the nature and number of rotors and the wiring of the plugboard merely from studying the encrypted communications. They broke Enigma and other equally difficult codes and cyphers, and in doing so probably enabled the war to be won by the Allies.

Not all thinking has good outcomes. Failures to reason or to reason well can have unfortunate or even disastrous consequences. In 2013, Oscar Pistorius, the South African Olympic athlete, shot and killed his girlfriend Reeva Steenkamp through a closed toilet door. His immediate explanation, from which he never wavered, was that he had mistaken her for an intruder. Pistorius was chronically afraid of dangerous intruders and armed against them. On his account, he heard a noise in the bathroom, collected his gun, and told his girlfriend, believing her still to be in bed, to call the police. Entering the bathroom, he stated in court, 'Then I heard a noise from inside the toilet—what I perceived to be somebody coming out of the toilet. Before I knew it, I fired four shots through the door.' The police did not believe his intruder story and charged him with murder. However, after a lengthy trial the court accepted his explanation, and convicted him of culpable homicide or manslaughter instead. (An appeal court later changed this to a murder conviction on a legal point.) In this case, a false inference—of a dangerous intruder in his bathroom—had fatal consequences.

One kind of fatal inferential error that occurs every day is misdiagnosis of a patient's medical condition. It is estimated that between 40,000 and 80,000 patients per year die in US hospitals due to diagnostic errors. There are many reasons for such errors to occur. They are more likely when a patient's symptoms are ambiguous and could represent different medical conditions. Errors may also occur due to overworked staff dealing with several emergency cases at the same time. However, it is likely that many of these mistakes are due to one or more of the *cognitive biases* that will be discussed in this book. Such biases have been heavily researched by cognitive and social psychologists and are fairly well understood. An example which might apply in medical diagnosis is *confirmation bias*. If the doctor thinks first of a particular diagnosis, she may then continue to look for evidence to support it and fail to seek (or notice) evidence that contradicts it. We know that such false diagnoses occur frequently as they can be detected during post-mortem examinations.

## Different kinds of reasoning

Philosophers distinguish between three main forms of inference: deduction, induction, and abduction. Abduction means 'reasoning to best explanation' and medical diagnosis is a good example of this. Such diagnosis is normally based on a combination of several forms of evidence: objectively measurable signs and symptoms

3

(e.g. blood tests), the patient's medical history, relevant risk factors (e.g. age, gender, family history), and an interview with the patient. Such inferences are generally probabilistic—the best explanation is the most probable, but not necessarily correct. Abductive inferences also occur in many other domains where we seek explanations. Suppose an airliner crashes into the ocean. Was this due to mechanical failure, pilot error, sabotage, or some other cause? Sometimes the cause may be established with very high confidence, but in other cases remains uncertain. Scientists are also called on frequently by the public to provide explanations for events, for example for the apparently inexorable increases in oceanic and climatic temperatures.

Abductive inferences are inherently uncertain and experts do not always get them right. For example, in 1996 the British government published a report, backed by leading scientists, suggesting a link between the eating of beef infected by BSE, or 'mad cow disease', and the emergence of a number of cases of a new form of CJD, the human variant. Since the British public had been exposed to meat containing the BSE prion for some years and as the symptoms were slow to emerge, a number of leading experts at the time suggested that we were seeing the tip of an iceberg. It was forecast that thousands more cases would emerge in the next few years. Naturally this caused some considerable panic, but the epidemic never occurred, with the numbers of CJD cases actually falling in the UK since this time. The abduction from new form CJD to BSE-infected meat was highly plausible but apparently wrong. I am not criticizing the experts here: it was the best explanation on the evidence available at the time. People are not always forgiving of expert misjudgements, however. Despite the fact that earthquakes are notoriously difficult to forecast, a group of scientists were convicted of manslaughter by a regional Italian court in 2012 and sentenced to six years in prison each. Their crime: giving false reassurances before an earthquake that killed over 300 people. This led to a mass protest by the international scientific community

and these extraordinary convictions were later overturned by
an appeal court.

Deductive or logical inferences are assigned an especially
important status by philosophers. The reason is that a logically
valid argument will guarantee a true conclusion given true
assumptions. Most mathematics can be regarded as a special
form of logic, in which theorems are deduced from axioms or
assumptions. A good example is Euclid's geometry, remarkably
published in 300 BC, which deduced all the main features of
elementary geometry as taught today. The system was based on
five basic assumptions or axioms such as (a) a straight line can be
drawn between any two points, (b) all right angles are equal, and
(c) parallel lines never meet. In logical systems there are always
some things postulated or assumed from which everything else
is deduced. These axioms are typically intuitive and cannot
themselves be proved. If there is a limitation, it is here that it
will be found. For example, Euclid's axioms apply to flat but not
curved surfaces, such as the surface of the Earth. Some of his
axioms do not hold in this case, rendering his theorems false, so
that a different system of geometry is required for curved surfaces
and spaces.

If we think of this kind of inference in everyday argument, we can
see that the same problem arises. Even if someone's reasoning is
sound, we may not agree with their conclusions because we do not
accept their premises. That is why political arguments may appear
futile or irresolvable. Typically, such debates take place between
people with different belief systems. Suppose the argument is
about abortion. One side takes the view that a woman's right to
control her own body is axiomatic, but the other side starts with
the assumption that the right to life is absolute and applies to a
foetus, no matter how young. Given these starting points, the two
sides will inevitably draw opposite conclusions about the practice
of abortion. No amount of logical reasoning will resolve their
argument. Logic works best in scientific domains where people

can agree on some basic assumptions and practices. But even in science such agreement is not always possible, and a field may divide into those following different methods or paradigms, at least until overwhelming evidence is found to support one position or the other.

If we only had deductive inference to call on, then we could never learn anything new. Deductions merely bring out conclusions that follow from what we already believe or assume to be true. If we believe that all cats have tails and learn that our neighbours have a new cat called Fluffy, then we can deduce that Fluffy has a tail. But how did we come to believe that all cats have tails to start with? We might have been taught this, like a scientific law, but more likely we learned this from experience when we were children. This is where inductive inference comes into play. A child will encounter dozens if not hundreds of cats when growing up and (normally) all will be seen to have a tail. To infer that all cats have tails from these observations is an induction. Such inferences are not logically valid (there may be cats without tails that we have not seen) but they are very useful. Of course, some cats for reasons of breeding or accident do not actually possess a tail, so the generalization is not strictly correct. But this is the nature of most general rules we acquire from experience. If they mostly hold, they are still very useful forms of knowledge, which is why we seem to have evolved to learn in this way.

The psychological study of thinking is as old as psychology itself, with the first systematic experiments reported in the 19th century. Thinking was a mainstream topic for university psychology courses even in the early part of the 20th century, well before anyone had heard of cognitive psychology or neuropsychology. There is good reason for this. Psychology branched off from philosophy, and philosophers from Aristotle onwards were interested in trying to understand and explain human thinking. It is, after all, the main tool of their trade. The ancients also believed, as most psychologists still do today, that it is thinking—or more accurately a certain kind of thinking—that separates human intelligence from that of all other animal species. Animals generally learn to adapt their behaviour on the basis of what has been successful in the past. Only humans can imagine the future, or alternative futures, and then calculate the course of action needed to ensure the best outcome.

This *Very Short Introduction* is called *Thinking and Reasoning* because most of the kinds of thinking studied by contemporary psychologists involve thinking that computes some kind of outcome and can be described as one or another kind of reasoning. However, I could not just call the book 'Reasoning', as I also cover topics such as intuition and insight which do not clearly qualify as such. Historically, the definition of thinking has developed from one originally based on the contents of our consciousness towards the modern idea of computation. I will provide a brief outline of how this came about.

## Early studies by the introspection method

You may believe, as Aristotle did, that thinking refers to the contents of your conscious mind. For example, if you are with a group of friends, 'lost in thought' and obviously not paying attention, someone might ask you what you were thinking. You will have a memory of recent thoughts, images, or words that you can use to answer the question, should you choose to do so. Of course, we regard such thoughts as private and accessible only to ourselves. If what we were actually thinking was that the enquirer had put on a lot of weight, or that his wife was having an affair behind his back, we would be unlikely to give a truthful answer. But in principle we can, it seems, report on our conscious thoughts. Philosophers used the introspective method from Aristotle onwards to study thinking. They studied the only mind to which they had direct access—their own.

When psychology emerged as a separate discipline in the 19th century it was based on the systematic study of human behaviour, using the experimental method when possible. This posed immediate problems for the traditional method of introspection. Scientific method requires that observations be objective and repeatable. How can introspection be verified by an independent observer? Early experiments, such as the studies carried out at the University of Wurzburg in Germany around 1900, used trained 'introspectionists'. It was supposed that linking a stimulus to a response should be some conscious and reportable thought or imagery. For example, if I give you a word association test and you answer 'leaves' when I say 'tree' you might report that you saw an image of a tree with leaves on. Sometimes this is what occurred, but on other occasions the trained observers reported nothing at all in their minds linking the words, or else vague feelings that could not be described. The clear suggestion here is that thought may not always be consciously accessible.

One of the great founding fathers of psychology, William James, was worried that people could only report their thoughts as memories of something past and that introspection was itself a mental act. Asking someone to report their thoughts would surely change what they were thinking. But the greatest early insight into the problems of trying to study one's own thinking came from Sir Francis Galton. Born in 1822, Galton was a half-cousin of Charles Darwin. He was a most prodigious researcher and writer across a variety of sciences, carrying out particularly important work in psychology, statistics, and genetics. Among many other topics, he carried out important studies on the nature of thinking, using himself as the subject of study.

While Galton studied his own thinking, he claimed to have solved the problem raised by James as follows: 'It would seem impossible to give the required attention to the processes of thought and yet think freely as if the mind had been in no way preoccupied. The peculiarity of the experiments I am about to describe is that

8

I have succeeded in evading this difficulty. My method consists in allowing the mind to play freely for a brief period, until a couple or so ideas have passed through it, and then...to turn attention upon them...to scrutinise them, and to record their exact appearance.' This subjective assertion of validity reads strangely to a modern psychologist, but the results of his experiments are well worth noting.

Philosophers from Aristotle onwards had proposed that thinking consists of an *association of ideas* that occur in sequence in the mind. For this reason, early introspective experiments, including Galton's, focussed on associations. Most of his experiments involved word association tests administered repeatedly to himself, with the associations that came to mind carefully recorded. However, he first describes a walk down Pall Mall in London, in which he estimates that he observed around 300 objects, taking only mental note of the thoughts that came to mind. In his words, 'It was impossible for me to recall in more than the vaguest way the numerous ideas that had passed through my mind but of this, at least, I was sure, that samples of my whole life had passed before me...I saw at once that the brain was vastly more active than I had previously believed it to be.' He was less impressed, however, when he repeated the walk and found that many of the associations were the same: 'The actors in my mental stage were indeed very numerous but not so numerous as I had imagined.' This frequent repetition of thought was confirmed more rigorously in his word association experiments in which all associations were formally recorded.

Galton's more profound observation, however, was that the production of these ideas was automatic, operating beneath the level of conscious thought: 'The more I have examined the working of my own mind...the less respect I feel for the part played by consciousness...Its position appears to be that of a helpless spectator of but a minute fraction of a huge amount of automatic brain work.' While Galton's experiments belong to a

9

bygone era, this conclusion is remarkably modern and few contemporary psychologists would disagree with it. The thoughts of which we are conscious do indeed represent very little of the work that the brain carries out. And herein lies the key limitation of the introspective method: we do not have access to how our minds work simply by studying our own consciousness.

## The influence of Freudian theory

Sigmund Freud was an Austrian doctor, born in 1856, who specialized in the treatment of mental illness, especially neurosis. To this end, he developed the practice of *psychoanalysis*, in which a therapist talks to a patient over many sessions, in order to discover the underlying causes of their condition. This would now be classified as a form of psychotherapy. What makes it distinctive is the theory which lies behind it, for which Freud is particularly famous. It may be surprising to learn that Freudian theory plays little part in the teaching of psychology today. A student might take a whole undergraduate degree without encountering it at all. If it is mentioned, it will probably be in a course on the history of psychology. The reason for this is that modern psychology is dominated by the scientific method, in which theories must be tested empirically, preferably by controlled experiments. A scientific theory must, in principle, be open to falsification. Psychologists do not regarded Freudian theory as scientific in this sense. How, for example, could you test whether a psychoanalytic interpretation of a dream is actually true?

Freudian theory has been and remains vastly influential in literature and culture, as well as in psychotherapy. It is also an important part of the history of psychology and certainly influenced ideas about thinking. If thinking is the flow of consciousness, as was generally believed for some 2,000 years, then the mind is conscious. But Freud—and other psychoanalysts—argued that our behaviour is often controlled by an unconscious or preconscious mind. Like Galton, but for entirely different reasons, Freud believed that consciousness was the tip of the iceberg. His primary interest was in the treatment of mental disorders such as free-floating anxiety, phobias, and obsessive-compulsive behaviours. As is well known, the Freudian unconscious is the repository of repressed emotions which can lead to irrational behaviours. Associated with repression are defence mechanisms, like projection and rationalization. For example, a person might avoid attending a meeting which requires revisiting the scene of a traumatic incident, whose memory has been repressed. If asked why, they will claim that they are too busy or not feeling well. According to Freud, such explanations would be *rationalizations*: false reasons invented by the conscious mind to explain behaviour caused by the unconscious.

The idea that people may rationalize unconsciously caused behaviour has been retained in modern psychology, but without the rationale in terms of repressed emotion. Indeed, I have made use of this idea myself in my work on dual-process theory discussed later in this book. In one famous experiment, published in the 1970s, participants were asked to choose between four pairs of pantyhose laid out left to right, on the basis of quality. People had a marked preference for the right-hand pair, explaining that it had better qualities—strength, elasticity, etc. No one said they chose them because they were on the right. The only problem is that all four pairs were identical. This shows us that (a) people are not conscious of the positional bias the experiment shows, and (b) that they rationalize behaviour caused by this unconscious bias. But note that contrary to Freudian theory, this rationalization is not a defence mechanism. It is implausible to think that any repressed emotions are in play here, certainly for the great majority of participants. But the fact that people can happily rationalize explanations for their own behaviour is another black mark for the introspective method.

We all have common-sense views about our behaviour and that of others, sometimes termed 'folk psychology'. The idea that we can provide explanations for our own behaviour is one such belief. It must be, because there is an opinion-polling industry based upon it. Pollsters not only ask people how they are going to vote in an election, for example, but also *why*. Or they ask how their opinions have been changed by recent events. There are many psychological studies which suggest that the answers to such questions will be unreliable. Folk psychology may hold that people act for conscious reasons which they can report, but the scientific evidence suggests otherwise. The tricky side of this is that people don't know what they don't know! One of the basic rules of psychology is that people will answer any damn silly question you put to them. That does not mean you should believe the answers.

## Behaviourism

Early in the 20th century, a movement called *behaviourism* was founded in strong reaction against introspective psychology. Behaviourism banished any reference to the internal workings of the mind and was to dominate psychology for the best part of fifty years. The rationale was clear. Psychology is a science and as such must rely on objective observations which can be repeated by another observer. On this basis, we can only study behaviour and not mental states. As the old joke goes, when two behaviourists meet, one says 'How am I?' and the other replies 'You are fine. How am I?' Behaviourism, in different forms, dominated psychology for the first half of the 20th century.

The school of behaviourism was founded by John B. Watson, born in South Carolina in 1878. In a famous essay published in 1913, Watson launched a strong attack on introspective psychology: 'Psychology as the behaviourist views it is the prediction and control of behaviour. Introspection forms no essential part of its methods... The time seems to have come when psychology must discard all reference to consciousness; when it need no longer delude itself into thinking that it is making mental states the object of observation.' In common with later behaviourists,

Watson was very interested in the study of animal learning, proposing that human and animal behaviour are controlled by the same mechanisms.

Early behaviourists focussed on *classical conditioning*. When a stimulus and response are associated *and* reinforcement (reward or punishment) is present, the association will be learned. Thus a rat may be trained to run away from a red light if it is given an electric shock when the light shines. A behaviourist would argue that a human phobia is learned in exactly the same way. For example, a person who experiences severe turbulence when flying may refuse to board an aircraft in future. But the behaviourist would make no reference to an emotional experience like fear, stating instead that the avoidance of flight was a conditioned response. Thus psychology was rendered 'scientific' by restricting its terminology to objective observation.

Perhaps the best known of the behaviourists was the American psychologist B. F. Skinner (1904–90). He emphasized what is known as operant or instrumental conditioning. Behaviours may be produced randomly but only those that are rewarded will persist, meaning that an individual's behaviour becomes shaped or adapted to its environment. Skinner was easily the most famous psychologist of his time and even wrote a novel called *Walden Two*, depicting his view of a utopian society built around operant conditioning. Skinner met his match, however, when he wrote a book attempting to explain the acquisition of human language as the conditioning of 'verbal behaviour'. A young and then little-known linguist called Noam Chomsky wrote one of the most important book reviews in the history of psychology, tearing Skinner's arguments to pieces. Chomsky, who went on to become the world's most famous and influential linguist, showed that language has a structure which could not be acquired by Skinnerian learning. This was one of several key influences which led people to understand the inadequacy of behaviourist learning theory.

Behaviourism dominated psychology up until the late 1950s, which is surprising given its limitations. In particular, the suggestion that human behaviour can be explained in the same way as that of other animals is patently false. For example, humans have a remarkably advanced system of language which, as Chomsky showed, cannot simply be described as 'verbal behaviour'. Humans can also perform cognitive feats that no kind of conditioning can explain. I refer here to everyday ordinary humans, not geniuses. For example, suppose you live in one part of London and invite someone who lives in another district to come to dinner. You give them—using language—just the following information: house number, street name, postcode, time, and date. Barring accidents, most people will find their way at approximately the right time, even though they have never visited that area before. In doing so, they make numerous decisions such as which tube train to catch, at which station to leave the train, and which of a number of different street turnings to take as they walk to a house. Their journey is unique, so there is no relevant conditioning of the stimulus–response kind. It is evident that no other animal on the planet could perform such a feat or any of its essential components, such as understanding language, reading maps, or calculating in advance the time of the journey. To deal with such things, a completely new approach was needed.

## Cognitive psychology

Cognitive psychology is a movement which started around 1960 and within ten years or so had largely displaced behaviourism. It is still the dominant paradigm for the study of thought, although its methods have sometimes been supplemented in recent years by those of neuroscience, allowing brain processes to be tracked while people perform cognitive tasks. Scientific thinking is often dominated by analogies; for example, Watson proposed that the brain was like a telephone switchboard with incoming stimuli wired directly to outgoing responses. Cognitive psychology arose

Thinking and Reasoning

from the advance of digital computing and the powerful metaphor it provided. Computers process information in accordance with sets of instructions—or programs—with which they are supplied.

The premise of cognitive psychology is that the brain is a computer and our task is to uncover its programs. When you give me an address and I turn up for dinner at the right time that is a response to a stimulus. But in between, there must be a great deal of mental activity in the form of information processing by the brain. No robot equipped with the smartest computers could conceivably perform this task at present, but we assume that it could eventually, with the right programming. We humans already have this software! Trying to make computers and robots smart and trying to understand how human intelligence works are complementary activities. Together they form what is known as cognitive science.

The study of the human mind has re-entered psychology in a different form than that which preceded behaviourism. Thinking is no longer seen as a flow of consciousness, but rather as a high-level form of information processing in the brain. To be sure, consciousness is still a puzzle and a subject for study, but it is no longer viewed as the essential stuff of the mind, and nor is introspection the methodology preferred by cognitive psychologists. What we do is perfectly scientific and not that different from the method of physics. In both disciplines, we observe the observable and theorize about the unobservable processes responsible. For example, a gravitational field is a theoretical construct to explain the observed behaviour of objects of different masses in spatial proximity to each other, such as the stars in a galaxy. Theories of gravitation are tested by the predictions they make about the movements of objects. In the same way, we study thinking by theorizing about the mental processes involved, and making predictions about behaviour. For example, we predict that one problem should be harder to solve than another, as measured by errors or response times.

The theories refer to processes that are not observable, but they can still be tested by their observable effects on our behaviour.

What, then, is thinking as viewed by a modern cognitive psychologist? Any cognitive task involves a multitude of internal processes such as those involved in generating or understanding language, perceiving stimuli, or moving a finger to signal a 'yes' or 'no' response to a task as instructed. By 'thinking', we refer to the highest level of these processes and the most flexible. Thinking arises when there is no simple neurological programming or previously learned response that will deal with the current task. The psychology of thinking deals primarily with novelty. How do we solve a problem, make a decision, or reason to a conclusion when we have never encountered a task of that kind previously? Cognitive psychologists have been studying such questions intensively over the past fifty years or more and this book will summarize many of their findings.

# Chapter 2
# Problem solving

We have a problem to solve whenever we want to do something, but lack the immediate means to achieve it. Most of the goals we reach in our everyday life do not require problem solving because we have a habit or some prior knowledge that allows us to achieve them. Getting to work, for example, requires a series of decisions and actions that might be quite complex but are generally routine and executed automatically. We know how to start our cars, which route to drive, and so on. But if the car will not start one morning, or our usual route is blocked, *then* we have a problem to solve. Like many real world problems these are *ill-defined*, lacking clear procedures or rules for their solution. For example, if the car will not start, a variety of strategies and solutions may be tried. If the battery is flat, we may jump-start it from another car. Or we may borrow a car from a partner or friend, or decide to use public transport.

Ill-defined problems may be quite easy for a human to solve but would be next to impossible for a computer, unless it knew all the things that we know. By contrast, some problems—including many studied by psychologists—are *well-defined*. This means that there is a clear set of rules that can be applied to get from where you are to where you want to be. Artificial problems usually have this nature. Examples would be an anagram to solve (which we may encounter in doing a crossword), a sudoku puzzle, or a chess problem which requires you to find a checkmate in three moves. If a problem is well-defined, a computer program can in principle be written to solve it.

Problem solving is clearly a key feature of human intelligence. Animals have generally evolved with fixed behaviour patterns. Some of the things they do may seem very clever. For example, birds and other animals may migrate thousands of miles, arriving (usually) in the right place. Honey bees can signal the location of nectar to their fellow creatures using a sophisticated code. Predator animals follow complex strategies to trap their prey, and so on. But these behaviours have been acquired slowly through evolution and cannot be varied by the individual animal. If the environment changes, it will not be possible for an individual to adapt its behaviour. While there is some evidence of intelligent use of tools to solve novel problems in some animals, the solution of novel problems is what generally marks our species out as different from both animals and earlier hominids. Neanderthals had very sophisticated skills—in manufacturing tools and hunting prey, for example—but these skills were isolated from each other. Hence, they could not adapt their tool making if different kinds of prey were encountered. By contrast, our own species, *Homo sapiens sapiens*, was able rapidly to adapt the design of artefacts to achieve changing goals, which is probably the reason that we are the only hominid species to make it to the present day.

Human intelligence does not, in the main, rely on behaviour patterns fixed by evolution, and nor does it depend on habit learning. Humans can and have solved a whole range of novel problems, which is why we have been able to develop such advanced technologies. If we want to understand human intelligence, then we need to study how it is that humans can solve both ill-defined and well-defined problems. Not all problems have a uniquely correct solution, but that does not mean that we should give them up. For example, no human or machine can guarantee to compute the best chess move in most positions, but they can certainly identify moves that are much better than others. Our best scientists are like grandmasters, because science also cannot provide knowledge that is certainly true. Even great scientific theories, like Newton's mechanics, can be later shown to be incorrect or limited in certain respects. In Newton's case, the inaccuracies cannot be detected in systems moving much slower than the speed of light, and Newton's physics was close enough to the truth to allow all manner of technologies to be developed using its principles.

## Gestalt psychology and the phenomenon of insight

In Chapter 1, I stated that behaviourism was the dominant movement in psychology for half a century (from around 1910 to 1960). In retrospect, this movement held the discipline back in some important ways. Behaviourists did not just deny the study of consciousness but restricted the subject in a much more significant respect. They tried to explain all human intelligence in terms of conditioning and habit learning, as though human behaviour could be explained simply by studying the learning of rats and pigeons. On this basis, all human problem solving would have to occur gradually by trial-and-error learning.

Fortunately, a major challenge to the behaviourist viewpoint was developed by a German school of psychology that was also strong in the first half of the 20th century, known as Gestalt psychology. This important work in many ways anticipated the development of cognitive psychology in the 1960s, but without explicit reference to the concept of information processing. Most of the issues concerning human problem solving that are studied today were identified in this period. The term *gestalt* is used to refer to the idea of 'good form' or whole figure, whose properties cannot be deduced as the sum of its parts. Gestalt psychology was primarily concerned with the study of visual perception, but a number of leading scholars later applied their ideas to the study of thinking and problem solving, in direct conflict with behaviourism.

One major issue in this period focussed on whether problems were solved in a gradual or incremental manner (as claimed by behaviourists) or by a sudden and discontinuous *insight* (as argued by the Gestalt psychologists). Insight problems are those solved with a sudden 'Aha!' experience, although not all problems work this way of course. However, the discovery of insight problems shows that problem solving involves more than habit learning. An example is the nine dot problem shown in Figure 1. You may attempt to solve this, as I give the answer later.

In a famous monograph on problem solving, published posthumously in 1945, Karl Duncker laid out an important foundation of the modern study of the topic. The paper is mostly famous, however, for an ill-defined problem which has been the subject of much study since. Duncker framed the problem thus: 'Given a human being with an inoperable stomach tumour, and

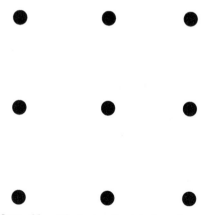

1. The nine dot problem. The instruction is to draw four straight lines, without lifting the pencil from the paper, such that the lines pass through all nine dots.

rays which destroy organic tissues at sufficient intensity, by what procedure can one free him of the tumour by these rays and at the same time avoid destroying the healthy tissue which surrounds it?' The solution which Duncker defined as correct was to focus the rays through a lens, so that they reached the critical density for destroying tissue only at the location of the tumour (see Figure 2). Participants found this difficult and only solved it after trying a number of different approaches.

In his studies of the tumour problem, Duncker developed a method of great importance in the subsequent study of problem solving, known as *verbal protocol analysis*. The participant is encouraged to 'think aloud' while trying to solve a problem, so that a record of thoughts, attempts, hypotheses considered, false solutions, and so on is available for the psychologist to study. It may seem, on first consideration, that this method is the same as introspective reporting, which I have said to be

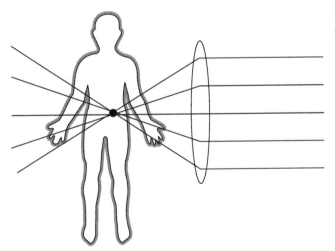

2. Solution to Duncker's tumour problem. Radiation is focussed through a lens on to the tumour, minimizing damage to surrounding tissue.

largely discredited. This matter has been much debated by psychologists, and the general view is that the two methods are *not* the same and that verbal protocol analysis is a lot more useful. Verbal protocols are produced concurrently and not retrospectively, and the participant is not being asked to explain or justify his or her actions. Hence, the burden of interpretation is on the psychologist, not the participant. Complex problem solving is almost impossible to study without this method, as we must have a record of intermediate outcomes to have any idea of the overall process.

Duncker showed the value of this method very well in his monograph. Some false solutions headed down blind alleys or violated the instructions (for example, expose the tumour by surgery when told it is inoperable). Others, however, developed part of the concept of the solution. For example, 'One ought to decrease the intensity of the rays on their way: for example—would this work?—turn the rays on at full strength only after the tumour has been reached.' Although the specific solution suggested here is impossible, the concept of reducing intensity of the rays on their way to the tumour does point towards the correct answer, which this participant eventually reaches with a classic sudden insight: 'Somehow divert...diffuse rays...disperse...stop! Send a broad and weak bundle of rays through a lens in such a way that the tumour lies at the focal point.' In more modern parlance introduced by post-war psychologists, the participant has made the problem easier by identifying a *subgoal*. A subgoal is one which, if reached, can then lead immediately to the goal. In this case, the subgoal is reducing the intensity of the rays on their way to the tumour.

Gestalt psychologists identified most of the key features and phenomena of problem solving, including the important distinction between insight and non-insight problems. They studied *incubation*, which is the phenomenon by which the solution to a difficult problem might appear in consciousness after a break in which one is thinking of other things, or sleeping. They identified the problem of mental *set* (now colloquially referred to as 'mindset'), in which one approaches a problem with a fixed set of assumptions which may be wrong and inhibit solution. A good example is the nine dot problem presented earlier in Figure 1. Most people, influenced by the gestalt perception of 'square' which the nine dots present, initially believe that they must confine the four lines within the square. With this set, the problem is impossible. Insight depends on realizing that the instructions place no such restriction. Without it, the solution is easy (see Figure 3). As both Gestalt psychologists and later researchers have shown, insight problem solving often requires giving a hint to help people restructure the problem. Popular culture now embodies

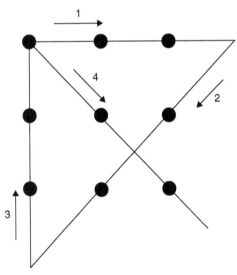

3. A solution to the nine dot problem. Starting with the pencil in the top left corner, draw a line to the right through and beyond the top row. Then diagonally down through two dots, back to the top corner through the left hand column, and down diagonally through the remaining two dots.

this idea with the prevalence of such phrases as 'think outside the box' or 'think laterally'.

Gestalt work also had educational implications. In a famous work entitled *Productive Thinking*, Wertheimer showed that rote learning, favoured by behaviourists, could lead to 'blind' thinking, lacking in insight. Wertheimer introduced another important method known as a *transfer* test. The area of a parallelogram can be proven to be the length of the base multiplied by the vertical height. Figure 4(a) shows a parallelogram with the vertices A, B, C, and D. It can be proven that it has the same area as the square ABFE as the triangles ACE and BDF are congruent. But if the method involves rote learning of instructions such as 'extend the base line to the right' and 'drop a vertical line from the top

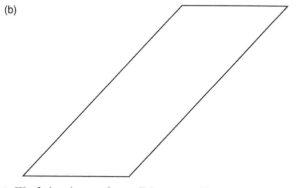

4. Wertheimer's area of a parallelogram problem.

left hand corner', it provides no insight. Wertheimer showed that children taught in this way will not be able to solve the problem for the parallelogram shown in Figure 4(b). A different method would be to give children parallelograms as paper cut-outs. Now, with a pair of scissors, they could cut off the triangle ACE and move it into the position of BDF, making a rectangle. This would provide insight which would survive the test of transfer to the differently arranged parallelogram in Figure 4b.

## Well-defined problems and the computational approach

In theory, a computer program can be written to solve any well-defined problem, provided it has an unlimited amount of time available. A modern computer can easily play a perfect game of Scrabble because it has time to compute all possible means of laying the tiles on the board and can quickly check whether each letter string is a legal word, using its built-in dictionary. On the other hand, a computer cannot play a perfect game of chess or bridge because there are far too many possible positions and sequences arising in these games for it to compute and evaluate all of them. Such problems are described as being *computationally intractable*, meaning that they are beyond the computational power of contemporary machines, as well as people.

Computational intractability is exploited by modern encryption systems. Secure computer systems, such as those used for online financial transactions, rely on encryption techniques which use both a public key included with the message (changed each time) and a private key held by the sender and receiver. The actual key used to encrypt the message can easily be computed from public and private keys in combination. The clever part, however, is that the public key is the product of two very large prime numbers which you have to factorize in order to break the code, unless you have the private key. There is no known quick method of computing factors of such a large number. So although one can easily write a computer program to solve this well-defined problem, even the fastest of modern computers might take hundreds or thousands of years to break the code.

Cognitive psychology is based on treating the mind as a computer and has theoretical links with the study of artificial intelligence, whose aim is to make computers smart. A pioneering research programme which engaged both objectives was that of Alan Newell and Herb Simon, mostly conducted in the 1960s, and focussed on human problem solving. They wrote a computer program called General Problem Solver that was designed to be intelligent. Traces of the computer's processes were compared with verbal protocols from humans solving the same problems, and showed striking similarities. Computers had so little power at that time that the software had to use more human-like methods. Modern computer programs can use 'brute force' methods which involve examining billions of possibilities, but these are of little psychological interest.

Newell and Simon described problem solving as a search within a *problem space*. A problem space is the set of possibilities generated by any well-defined problem. A computationally intractable problem is one with a very large problem space. In early and middle game positions in chess, for example, there are approximately thirty legal moves available to either side. This means that the number of chess positions that can be reached with ten moves on either side is around $30^{20}$—a vast number. So the search space for chess quickly becomes very large even if you only look a few moves ahead for either side. Even modern computers have to compromise breadth (number of alternative moves examined in a given position) against depth (number of moves calculated ahead of the current position). Modern programs will typically examine four moves in each position, with four replies, and so on, to considerable depth. This brute force method has enabled them to play to the standard of human grandmasters, but obviously not with the same strategy. As the great chess champion Gary Kasparov has observed, computers can find moves that grandmasters miss, but the reverse is true as well.

Newell and Simon suggested that both humans and computers needed intelligent methods to reduce the search space, and called these *heuristics*. Heuristics cannot guarantee success but they can lead to effective solutions to problems that are otherwise computationally intractable. One method is to work backwards from the desired solution to the current state, creating a subgoal, as discovered in Duncker's work. Another is *means–ends analysis*, where one calculates the difference between the current state and the goal state and tries to reduce that difference. For example, if you want to make an omelette, you need eggs. If there are none in the house, then you create a subproblem of obtaining eggs. If you solve this (e.g. by buying or borrowing) then you have moved closer to the solution state (a cooked omelette on your plate). In such real cases, of course, we might decide that the bigger problem is having lunch and that it may be easier to cook something else than find eggs. Newell and Simon's own artificial computer programs were able to prove many (but not all) theorems in mathematical logic using these heuristic methods—a very impressive achievement with the computer technology of that time.

It is clear from Newell and Simon's work and many later studies that people do indeed use heuristics to help solve problems with large problem spaces. There are many heuristics that humans can use when faced with difficult problems but they will not necessarily be applied consciously. Heuristics can operate in an intuitive or perceptual manner, as when strong chess players just 'see' better moves than weaker players. This comes from a great deal of experience, however, and is a kind of insight, as potential solutions are perceived without any process of conscious reasoning. Heuristics can also be explicit rules that can be taught to people to aid their problem solving. For example, if you are trying to solve an anagram, it is helpful to look for familiar letter strings. Say you have a ten-letter anagram but notice that it contains an 'i', 'n', and 'g'. You could suppose that it is a word ending in 'ing'. This might be wrong, of course, but for the time being you have reduced a ten-letter anagram to one of seven letters which is much easier to solve. If the anagram is contained in a crossword clue you can also try to determine the meaning of the solution word, which should help you to tell if this heuristic is likely to work.

Well-defined problems can be difficult because they have a large search space, like finding a good chess move. But they can also be hard for a different kind of reason: they may have a compelling but wrong intuitive solution. This was demonstrated quite recently in a short test of thinking devised by Shane Fredericks, who presented several problems whose solution can easily be computed, but which also have a competing and wrong intuitive answer. A good example is the bat and ball problem:

A bat and ball together cost $1.10. If the bat costs one dollar more than the ball, how much does the ball cost?

The correct answer—5 cents—can easily be deduced with some elementary algebra. But the incorrect answer—10 cents—comes directly to mind and people often give this without thinking. Many bright and well-educated people get this problem wrong, but not because the right answer is difficult to compute. There is now much evidence that relying on intuition with this kind of problem is a personality characteristic, meaning that some people are consistently likely to make this kind of error, while others check their intuitions by reasoning. This is related to what is now known as 'dual-process theory', which is very fashionable in contemporary psychology. The theory distinguishes between thought based on 'Type 1' processes (rapid and intuitive) and 'Type 2' processes (slow and reflective). It seems that we sometimes rely on the former when the latter are needed to solve a problem.

## Insight and expertise in problem solving

Insight problems have remained a focus for psychological research to the present day. The phenomenon of sudden solutions accompanied by an 'Aha!' experience, discovered by Gestalt psychologists, is of great psychological interest. In the computational approach, problem solving proceeds by the more or less systematic search of problem spaces. But clearly this does not explain the difficulty of insight problems, which are typically insoluble as people originally understand and represent them. Insight depends on restructuring problems to get rid of false assumptions and unhelpful mental sets. But how does this occur? The older studies tell us that it can happen spontaneously or be facilitated by small hints, which may not even be consciously noticed. But this does not help us very much in understanding the phenomenon.

We have known for some time that one means of solving insight problems is to reason by analogy. One more recent study of Duncker's tumour problem provided some of the participants with a prior story about a general attacking a well-guarded fort. The fort can be approached from four separate directions and the general decides to split his forces and approach from all directions simultaneously, converging on the fort with maximum strength. This is what is known as a structural analogue of the tumour problem. The domain is military rather than medical, but it involves the idea of distributing weak forces which only converge for maximum strength at the location of the target. People who are given this story are better able to solve the tumour problem, but most still require a hint that the general story is relevant. Creative thinking often requires people to connect ideas from quite different domains. A good example is the reflective lens universally used on roads to allow car drivers to see unlit road markings at night. These are often referred to as cats' eyes, a source of inspiration for their inventor, Percy Shaw. He realized that if a cat's eye reflected light at night allowing one to see it, then an artificial lens could serve the same function for drivers.

A major issue for contemporary researchers is whether insight problem solving involves some distinctive psychological or neurological process. The opposing camps are known as 'business as usual' and 'special process'. The former argue that the cognitive processes leading to insight are the same as those used generally to search problem spaces, differing only in the emotional experience of sudden solution. There is, however, good evidence to support the idea that insight involves a special and distinctive process. For example, brain imaging studies show that specific regions of the right cerebral cortex become activated when people report moments of insight. Special process theorists often make clear connections with dual-process theories of thinking, mentioned earlier. Although rapid and preconscious Type 1 processes have often been linked to cognitive biases—as with the bat and ball problem—there is no necessary reason to suppose that intuitive processes will result in errors. Intuitions can also be helpful, especially when the individual has relevant experience. Thus insight may reflect the operation of preconscious Type 1 processing.

This thought links us directly with another topic: expert problem solving. Type 2 reasoning abilities are known to be better developed in those of higher general intelligence. You might think that this means that experts are more intelligent, but this is to misunderstand the nature of expertise. Although a minimum level of IQ may well be needed to become expert in some fields, what marks experts out is the extent of specialized knowledge that they have acquired. This knowledge is often manifest in the form of superior intuitions or Type 1 processes, as with master chess players who just 'see' stronger chess moves. Studies of expert problem solving generally show that experts rely on *pattern recognition*. From experience, they recognize situations that are similar to those seen before and can rapidly propose potential solutions that have worked in the past. Only when problems are unusually novel do they need to engage in explicit reasoning of a Type 2 nature. This is exactly how we would want it to be. If an experienced doctor is dealing with a medical emergency, or a pilot encounters hazardous weather during a flight, we do not want them to spend a lot of time reasoning things out from first principles. On the contrary, we want our experts to be able to recognize problems and react quickly.

Gary Klein has carried out many studies of how experts solve problems and make decisions in their workplace, and emphasizes precisely this intuitive aspect of expertise. He tells a story of a commander in the US fire service, who led his men into a one-storey house to put out a fire. After an unsuccessful attempt to extinguish it, he developed a feeling that something was not right and evacuated his men. Shortly after, the floor on which they had been standing collapsed into a fire blazing in the basement below. While the commander claimed a 'sixth sense' had saved them from dying in the fire, Klein provided a more mundane explanation. The commander did not know that there was a basement in the building, but the fire did not respond as expected and the room was too hot based on his experience. In this case the pattern was *not* recognized and the lack of fit was what created his unease and his (wise) decision to withdraw.

In summary, research on problem solving shows that there is more to it than reasoning or computing solutions to well-defined problems. Some problems are hard because there are too many possibilities to consider and some short-cut means must be found to solve them. Others are hard because we simply lack the right approach and mental set and may only solve them when a rest, a hint, or an analogy enables us to gain insight. Problems that are difficult for a novice may be easy for an expert, because the latter has so much knowledge and experience that they can recognize a familiar pattern. We have also had our first encounter with dual-process theory and can see that fast, intuitive processes can be both a source of error and a cause of success, depending on the context and the prior knowledge of the problem solver.

# Chapter 3
# Thinking hypothetically

A remarkable and distinctive feature of human intelligence is our ability to think hypothetically. We can imagine how things might be in the future and how they might have turned out differently in the past. Such are our powers of imagination that we enjoy reading novels and watching dramas on TV or in the cinema, an extraordinary demonstration in itself of the unique form of human intelligence. Imagination is not just there for entertainment, however. It plays an important role in science, arts, and engineering, and is fundamental to rational decision making.

A hypothesis is a supposition about some aspect of the world about us. Developing and testing hypotheses in an informal way is part of our everyday thinking. If our car will not start in the morning and we have some rudimentary knowledge of mechanics, we may think of the most common cause: a flat battery. This hypothesis can quickly be eliminated if the engine turns over in a healthy manner when we turn the key but fails to fire. In this case, I know enough to think that the problem is either some kind of fuel starvation or an ignition failure. I also know enough to hand the car over to a mechanic at this point to find and fix the fault. We can see here that hypothesis testing is part of problem solving. The problem is that the car won't go and needs to be fixed. Identifying the cause of the problem, however, is the first stage in solving it. The mechanic is not going to waste time stripping fuel lines looking for a blockage without first performing a simple test on the ignition system. It could be dirty spark plugs that are responsible and it is quick and easy to check.

Here we can introduce the idea of a *mental model*. All car drivers have a representation of a motor car in their minds which tells them how it works. Generally, the model is fairly simple, involving such rules as turning the ignition key starts the engine, pressing the accelerator pedal increases speed, pressing the brake reduces speed, and so on. Experts develop much more complex and detailed mental models, however. The car mechanic has a detailed mental model of what happens between the ignition key being turned and the engine starting, or between pressing the brake pedal and brakes being applied. The average driver has only a vague idea of these things or possibly none at all. My hypotheses when my car won't start are basically (a) flat battery (in which case I know what to do) or (b) some other cause (in which case I turn it over to the mechanic). The mechanic's more sophisticated mental model allows him or her to test a series of ever more specific hypotheses, converging efficiently on the cause of the problem.

The thought process in finding mechanical faults is similar to that involved in medical diagnosis, which goes something like this:

- Gather initial evidence (e.g. patient's symptoms) and form a hypothesis of the most likely condition consistent with it.

- Perform some test to see if the hypothesis is correct (e.g. examine patient, run blood test).

- If the evidence eliminates the first hypothesis then conjecture the next most likely cause and repeat the process.

Of course, both car mechanics and physicians are expert problem solvers, which means they rely a lot on recognition of familiar patterns and also have well-learned procedures for testing hypotheses. Psychological research on hypothesis testing, as with most topics in the psychology of thinking, has focussed mostly on untrained participants presented with novel problems, where reasoning is central. One reason this is considered important is because testing hypotheses plays an important role in scientific thinking.

## Hypothesis testing and scientific reasoning

The purpose of science is not simply to gather facts but to advance knowledge. Science depends upon having good theories, such as Newton's mechanics or Darwin's natural selection theory of evolution. Such theories allow us to understand and predict the natural world and are also the basis for technological advancement. Philosophers of science, however, have long been bothered by what is known as the *problem of induction*. Scientific laws are usually expressed as universal statements: 'all A are B'. An example is Boyle's law, which states that in a closed system the pressure of a gas is inversely proportional to its volume, provided that temperature remains constant. This applies to all gases in all circumstances. Such a law can clearly be tested experimentally. If we compress a mass of gas to half its volume (and hold temperature constant) we can predict that the pressure should double. An independent measurement of pressure can then confirm our prediction.

The philosophical problem with this method is that no matter how many experiments confirm it, we cannot conclude that Boyle's law is necessarily true. The law is not a logically valid inference from the evidence. However, as the philosopher Karl Popper pointed out, we only need one disconfirmation to know that it is *false*. If our scientific law has the form 'all A are B', we need find only one case of an A that is not a B to disprove it. And this conclusion *is* logically valid. So in principle, one experiment could refute the law. Hence Popper recommended that we construct scientific theories to be falsifiable and then set about trying to disprove them.

Popper's philosophy of science was extremely influential when published in the 1950s, and inspired a British psychologist called Peter Wason in some of his early experiments, published from the 1960s onwards. Wason had a very important influence on the psychology of reasoning as we know it today. He devised several novel tasks which are still used by investigators, and was one of the first psychologists to suggest that people may be biased and irrational in their reasoning. In particular, he suggested that people, or at least his student participants, were bad Popperians. They seemed to test their hypotheses by trying to make them true rather than false. This tendency has become known generally as *confirmation bias*. Wason's evidence was based on two tasks of his own invention, known as the 2-4-6 task and the selection task.

The 2-4-6 task was originally published in 1960 but its study has continued to the present day. Participants (usually students) are told that the experimenter has in mind a rule which classifies sets of three whole numbers, or triples. An example which conforms to this rule is 2-4-6. The task is to discover the rule by generating new triples: the experimenter will then say whether these conform to the rule or not. The participants were asked to record the reasons for each triple and only to announce the rule when they were sure they knew it. However, if they got it wrong, they were asked to continue with more tests until they gave up or a time limit was reached. The experiment has a trick, which makes it very difficult to solve the task. The actual rule is a very general one—*any ascending sequence*—but the example given suggests something much more specific, like numbers increasing with equal intervals. What happens is that people become convinced that a more specific rule is correct because all their tests get positive feedback. Here is an example protocol from the original 1960 study:

8 10 12 two added each time; 14 16 18 even numbers in order of magnitude; 20 22 24 same reason; 1 3 5 two added to previous numbers

*The rule is that by starting with any number two is added each time to form the next number (1)*

2 6 10 the middle number is the arithmetic mean of the other two: 1 50 99; same reason

*The rule is that the middle number is the arithmetic mean of the outer two (2)*

3 10 17 same number seven added each time; 0 3 6 three added each time

*The rule is that the difference between two numbers next to each other is the same (3)*

12 8 4 the same number is subtracted each time

*The rule is adding a number, always the same, to form the next number (4)*

1 4 9 any three numbers in order of magnitude

*The rule is any three numbers in order of magnitude (5)*

This participant keeps announcing incorrect rules, some of which are very similar, before eventually finding the solution. Note that every triple tested, including the final one, is a positive test of the current hypothesis. In other words, a case expected to belong to the rule. The final triple 1-4-9 would, however, be a *negative* test of all the preceding rules that were announced, such as adding the same number to form the next in the series. With that hypothesis, the experimenter should say no, it does not belong to the rule. The main finding of the study is that such negative tests are rarely made, and hence the hypotheses suggested by 2-4-6 are difficult or impossible to eliminate.

The 2-4-6 task shows that people mostly test their hypotheses with positive predictions, but does this mean they have a

**Table 1 Confirmatory and disconfirmatory results of positive and negative hypothesis testing**

|  | Conforms to the rule? | |
| --- | --- | --- |
| Hypothesis test | Yes | No |
| Positive | Confirms | Disconfirms |
| Negative | Disconfirms | Confirms |

confirmation bias, as Wason suggested? Examine Table 1. In principle, either a positive or negative test could lead to confirmation or disconfirmation. *On this particular task*, a positive test of the hypothesis cannot receive the answer 'No', but this is not true of hypotheses in general. If a gardener, observing the plants in a newly acquired plot, thinks that the soil is acid, she can carry out a pH test which will tell whether it is acid or alkaline. While the test is positive in attitude, the result can easily be negative, if the soil is actually alkaline. If her neighbour is convinced that the soil is alkaline and suggests the test, the result is the same. It does not matter which result was expected.

What do scientists actually do when their predictions are falsified by their experiments? Studies of real scientific groups suggest that theories and hypotheses are rarely abandoned when a disconfirmatory result is first encountered. Instead the experiment will be checked and often repeated. Only when repeated falsifications occur do they reject the hypothesis and revise the theory which led to it. As a scientist myself, I do not regard this as confirmation bias. Theories take a lot of time and effort to develop and are based on much evidence. When a prediction fails, it makes sense to check whether the experiment is at fault. But experiments can also rock established theories when they cannot be explained away. One such experiment was critical in the development of Einstein's relativity theory, as mentioned earlier in the book.

# The Wason selection task

The selection task, first published in 1966, is probably the most famous problem in the psychology of reasoning. It has been intensively researched and has led to a number of novel theoretical developments. It was, however, presented originally as a hypothesis-testing task, which Wason also thought would demonstrate a confirmation bias. It involves the little word 'if', which has fascinated me to the extent I have written many of my research papers, and also an entire book, about it. If is the word we use in everyday language to express hypotheses and to stimulate hypothetical thinking. We use this word both to advise (if you study hard, you will pass the examination) and to warn people (if you do not hurry, you will miss your flight) as well as persuade them (if you vote for party X, then your taxes will go down). We use it to express predictions directly (if it rains, the barbeque will be cancelled) and also intentions (if I am offered the job, I will accept it). Conditional statements also figure frequently in scientific hypotheses (if a child watches violent television, they will become violent themselves).

The original form of the Wason selection task used abstract materials such as letters and numbers, which seems to make it a pure test of reasoning. An example of the abstract selection task is shown in Figure 5. Most people say that the A card must be turned over and many also choose the 3 card. But the generally accepted correct answer is the A and the 7. The key is to think about what could make the rule *false*: clearly a card which has an A on one side and does *not* have a 3 on the other side. Turning over the A card could discover such a case, as could turning over a card which is not a 3, in this case the 7. The 3 card is irrelevant, because finding a card with an A and a 3 would be consistent with the rule but could not prove it to be true. The rule does not state that a 3 must have an A on the back. Hence only cards with an A and not a 3 are relevant.

There are four cards lying on a table. Each has a capital letter on one side and a single-digit number on the other side. The exposed sides are shown below:

The rule shown below applies to these four cards and may be true or false:

If there is an A on one side of the card, then
there is a 3 on the other side of the card

Your task is to decide those cards, and only those cards, that need to be turned over in order to discover whether the rule is true or false.

5. A standard abstract version of the Wason selection task.

Wason suggested that people had a confirmation bias, and you can see why. They are asked to test a conditional hypothesis, of the kind commonly used in science. The tests they actually make seem to be intended to confirm the rule rather than refute it. Protocol analysis supports this. People will say, 'I am turning over the A because a 3 on the back would make it true' and vice versa. However, as I discovered very early in my career, a small change to the wording produces a big problem for this account. Keep everything the same in Figure 5 except for the rule, which now reads:

If there is an A on one side of the card, then there is *not* a 3 on the other side of the card.

Again most people choose the A and 3 cards, which are now logically correct. With this rule, the one card that can falsify the rule has an A on one side and a 3 on the other. How do people explain these choices? Well now they say, for example, 'I am turning over the A because a 3 on the back would make it false'. This is very strange. Negatives usually make things more difficult, but here the negative version is solved easily and the correct reason given!

This effect was discovered shortly after the period in which Wason supervised my PhD in the early 1970s. We called it the *matching bias*, as people seem to choose cards which match the value named in the rule. We also suggested that the reasons people give for their choices are rationalizations. Recall that on the 2-4-6 task people often reformulate, using different words, very similar or even identical hypotheses to the ones that have just been rejected by the experimenter. And now, on the selection task, we find that people explain their choices in terms of verification or falsification, even though they are really choosing the matching cards. This led us to publish the first dual-process theory of thinking in the psychology of reasoning, suggesting that different kinds of thinking were responsible for the choices made (Type 1) than for the explanations offered (Type 2). Much later, I was able to show that matching bias is linked to the use of implicit negatives; for example, 7 standing for 'not 3'. If the cards are described as A, not A, 3, and not 3, the matching bias effect largely disappears.

In its standard form (Figure 5) the selection task is very difficult, with only 10–20 per cent of people solving it, depending on the population tested. The minority who do solve the problem have been shown to have unusually high general intelligence. But it has been known for many years that when the task is made realistic, rather than abstract, it may be much easier. A very easy version is shown in Figure 6 using a drinking age rule. Most people given this problem choose to turn over 'beer' and '17 years of age'. They correctly look for the case where someone is drinking beer and is under the required age.

It was later realized that the drinking age problem, and other realistic versions that make the problem easy to solve, are logically

On this task imagine that you are a police officer on duty. It is your job to ensure that people conform to certain rules. The cards in front of you have information about four people sitting at a table. On one side of a card is a person's age and on the other side of the card is what the person is drinking:

| | | | |
|---|---|---|---|
| Beer | Coke | 20 years of age | 17 years of age |

Here is a rule:

> If a person is drinking beer then that person must be over 18 years of age

Select the card or cards that you definitely need to turn over to determine whether or not they are violating the rule.

**6. A realistic version of the Wason selection task.**

different from the standard task. In the standard task, people check if a rule is true or false. With the drinking age rule, they check whether or not a rule has been followed. Instead of looking for a falsifying case, they look for a violator. This is an important part of what makes the problem easy. Realistic versions of the task that concern truth or falsity sometimes improve performance but much less reliably. But the effects of context are also very subtle. In one study, for example, the first two sentences in Figure 6 were removed so that people were given the drinking age rule to test, but without the police officer scenario. With this change, the task was as difficult as ever!

The realistic version of the selection task has been the basis for a number of major theoretical proposals in the psychology of reasoning. It seems that the easier versions are ones where we are asked to reason about permissions (like the drinking age rule) or obligations, e.g. 'If you enter this area, you must wear a hard hat'. It has been suggested by some authors that we have a specific ability to reason in such situations, but there is disagreement about whether this is learned in child development or provided by evolution. Other theorists have appealed to more general mechanisms related to how context affects the interpretation of language or the application of decision theory (discussed in Chapter 4). While there is no clear resolution to these arguments at present, we can safely say that no other task has inspired so much theoretical thinking about how people reason.

## Assessing the probability of hypotheses

Wason's tasks concern how people decide whether hypotheses are true or false. In the real world, however, there is much uncertainty. For example, in English common law jurisdictions, including the USA, juries are required to assess probabilities. In criminal cases, they must hold a strong (but not certain) degree of belief in the guilt of the accused before convicting them, while in civil litigation they must simply decide, on the balance of probabilities, which side is favoured by the evidence. In such cases the presentation of evidence is governed by strict rules. Outside of the courtroom, however, our beliefs in evidence may be manipulated by those with vested interests, as in the case of arguments over the extent to which climate change is an imminent threat, or created by human activity. How people assign credence to sources is an issue studied by social psychologists and beyond the scope of this book. However, there are also important cognitive studies of how people determine their belief in hypotheses.

To distinguish between hypotheses, we need to examine evidence. But not all evidence is equal: we need evidence that is *diagnostic*. Suppose I am introduced to a male US senator and am trying to figure out which political party he represents. I might think—he is wearing a suit, most Republican senators wear suits, so he is probably a Republican. But this would be fallacious reasoning, because most senators wear similar suits, whatever their political party. The suit wearing is not diagnostic evidence. But then I

**Table 2 Contingencies in a possible causal relationship**

|  | Potential effect ($e$) | |
| --- | --- | --- |
| Potential cause ($c$) | Present | Absent |
| Present | A | B |
| Absent | C | D |

notice that he is wearing a red tie and infer on this basis that he is probably a Republican. Here, I am on stronger ground: red is the Republican colour and red ties are more frequently worn by members of this party. In this case, the evidence is more diagnostic than the suit wearing.

People do not necessarily think very clearly about evidence, however. Suppose we are trying to judge whether some potential cause $c$ results in an effect $e$ by noticing how often they occur together or separately. There are actually four cases to consider (Table 2). If we think that $c$ is a cause for $e$ then we should attend to all four frequencies, A, B, C, and D shown in the table. In our senator problem, the frequencies for suit wearing might be:

A  Republican wearing suit: 98 per cent
B  Republican not wearing suit: 2 per cent
C  Democrat wearing suit: 95 per cent
D  Democrat not wearing suit: 5 per cent

Now we can see that people considering only A and B will make a wrong inference, because the probability of a Republican wearing a suit is only slightly higher than the probability of a Democrat senator doing so. Now consider the red tie evidence. The figures might be:

A  Republican wearing red tie: 30 per cent
B  Republican not wearing red tie: 70 per cent

C   Democrat wearing red tie: 5 per cent
D   Democrat not wearing red tie: 95 per cent

Now suppose that people had just been given information A in this case, that 30 per cent of male Republican senators wear red ties. They might argue that most Republicans do not wear red ties, so a senator wearing a red tie is probably not Republican. This would be an even worse fallacy! The relevant issue is whether wearing a red tie makes a senator more likely to be Republican, and it clearly does on these figures. But you need to look at all four frequencies to know this. Research on such problems reveals cognitive biases. For example, when given the frequencies and asked to judge whether $c$ causes $e$, people give most weight to A, followed by B, C, and D, in that order. The effect is similar to the positivity bias we saw when discussing the 2-4-6 problem and the matching bias in the selection task. People focus on the hypothesis 'Republican senators wear red ties' and think only about these attributes, rather than also considering what Democrats wear.

## Causal and counterfactual thinking

An important current topic in the psychology of thinking concerns the mental models we may construct to understand causality. Causal models can help us to disentangle causation from correlation. Suppose you notice that three variables tend to correlate with each other, for example how fit someone is, how much exercise they take, and a tendency to be anxious. There are actually three different kinds of causal model we could construct (Figure 7). One hypothesis to explain these correlations would be that anxious people worry about their health and so engage in more exercise. As a result they are fitter. This is a model of type (c) in Figure 7:

Anxious personality → physical exercise → fitness

But we could be wrong. It could be that for some reason taking exercise makes you anxious as well as fit: model (b); or it could

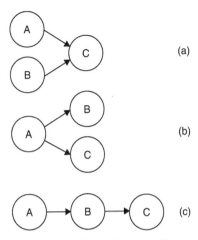

(a)

(b)

(c)

**7. Alternative causal models relating three variables.**

be that anxiety and exercise independently contribute to fitness: model (a). Testing such causal hypotheses requires *intervention*, which is the method of experimental science. Intervention involves systematically changing one of the variables. We might notice that people with yellow fingers are more likely to get lung cancer, but it is most unlikely that painting their fingers brown would improve their health! We are probably dealing with a model of type (b) where cigarette smoking causes both yellow fingers and lung cancer. Note in this case that yellow fingers are *diagnostic* of lung cancer, even though they have no causal role. That is, people with yellow fingers are more likely to have lung cancer. An intervention to prevent cigarette smoking should reduce both yellow fingers and cancer if this model is correct.

Popular culture is rife with false causal explanations. A popular expression in Britain (but not Finland) is 'it is too cold for snow'. In the British climate, two kinds of winter weather dominate, especially in the south: cold and clear, or mild and wet. So there is a negative correlation between precipitation and temperature.

Usually, when it feels very cold, the clouds stay away, hence this rather bizarre expression. Clearly it can and does snow when precipitation coincides with air temperatures close to or below freezing, so it is most often too warm to snow! Problem gamblers are often driven by misunderstanding probability and the false belief that they can intervene to change random events by the strategies they adopt. For example, 'systems' for playing roulette are based on the false premise that later bets can compensate for earlier losses. They cannot: each individual bet has a mathematically expected loss. Without special training our understanding of causation, correlation, and chance leaves much to be desired.

Finally, I should like to mention our extraordinary tendency to engage in counterfactual thinking. That is, thinking about how things might have worked out differently if something had been changed in the past. Counterfactual conditional statements occur frequently in everyday life, e.g. 'I would have had a great score today if I had holed some putts', 'Thatcher would never have been re-elected if Argentina had not invaded the Falkland Islands', or 'I would not be stranded here if I had had my car serviced'. We use these kinds of statements all the time, and they typically express (indirectly) a causal hypothesis. Counterfactual statements often imply more elaborated causal models, such as: 'Mrs Thatcher was unpopular but when the Argentinians invaded the Falklands Islands, she conducted a successful war, liberating the islanders. This boosted her popularity, enabling her to win the next general election.'

We also use counterfactual statements to undo past events in our minds, especially when we regret an outcome. Interestingly, we undo some events more than others. For example, we are more likely to regret an action than an inaction. If we hold on to a stock which later falls in price we will feel less regret than if we sell a stock which later rises in price. We are more likely to say 'if only I had not sold that stock' in the second case, than we are to say 'if only I had sold that stock' in the first. Similarly, if while driving home from work we decide to change our usual route and then hit a patch of oil and crash the car, we will say 'if only I had not changed my route'. Had the accident happened on our usual route, however, we would not regret our failure to change it. We also find it strangely easy to judge whether a counterfactual hypothesis is true or probable. Consider the statement:

If terrorists had not attacked New York in 2001 then the USA would not have invaded Iraq.

A lot of people will agree with this statement, without taking much time to think about it. But the events of 9/11 changed the world in so many different ways that the consequences of 'undoing' this event are clearly computationally intractable. This is not a difficulty for everyday hypothetical thinking, it seems! Even though Iraq was not responsible for the 9/11 attack, a person might argue that this event substantially changed American attitudes to war and the Middle East that can be seen as enabling an invasion which was motivated by other political factors. It seems that we naturally and easily construct such causal mental models for counterfactual scenarios, no matter how complex or incalculable they might seem to be.

In general, people test hypotheses by making positive predictions or looking for positive evidence to support them. We tend to neglect alternative hypotheses and negative evidence. However, research on the Wason selection task shows that we are much better at checking whether rules have been followed in more realistic contexts. In the real world we typically deal with uncertainty and have to try to determine how probable hypotheses are and whether one is more probable than another. Again, there are systematic biases in how we go about this, with typically incomplete searches for evidence. Causal hypotheses and mental models seem to be fundamental to our thinking, but our ability to distinguish correlation from causation without training is limited. We also have an extraordinary tendency to think counterfactually by mentally undoing past events, in order to envision alternative outcomes.

# Chapter 4
# Decision making

In a sense, we make a decision every time we do one thing when we could have done something else. However, by this definition we make thousands of decisions every day. Most of these are habitual and require little thought. Another view is that we make decisions when we depart from the habitual. For example, if we take a shower every morning then we are not deciding to do so by any process of reflective thinking. However, if we skip our shower because we are late for work then *that* requires a decision. Similarly, if the route we drive to work requires us to turn left at a junction, we would not want to call that decision making. It happens automatically with practice. Turning right instead, for a particular purpose—to post an urgent letter perhaps—would require a decision. And as we all know, it is quite likely that we will forget and turn left anyway. In the language of dual-process theory, automatic Type 1 processes dominate most of our everyday choices. The psychology of decision making mostly involves novel choice problems that require Type 2, deliberative thinking for their solution. Errors, however, are often attributed to Type 1 processing, as I will discuss in Chapter 7.

Hypothetical thinking is essential to deliberative decision making. That is because we have to imagine the consequences of our choices. Suppose a young man considers a choice between studying psychology or engineering at university. He imagines studying the two subjects and decides that psychology will be more interesting and enjoyable. If his thought experiment stops there, that will be his decision. But he might think further ahead to what happens after he graduates and perhaps do some web research on this. He notes that there is an excess of psychology graduates and that most will not find jobs in the subject. On the other hand, well-qualified engineers are in demand and are likely to have well-paid careers. On this basis, he may decide instead to study engineering. Part of his calculation is based on an assessment of risk. He believes that it is more probable that engineering will lead to a well-paid career and that this outweighs his interest in psychology.

The psychology of decision making has been much influenced by the study of economics, which provides a theory of rational decision making. The theory assumes that people do indeed project the consequences of their decisions, taking into account both the probability and the value to them of different outcomes. In the simplest case, these are just monetary values. Such choices can be represented in decision trees, of the kind shown in Figure 8. In this case, an investor has $100,000 which they can afford to tie up for five years. They have the opportunity to invest in a start-up company with great potential. If it succeeds, then they expect to double their money in five years. But they also recognize a 30 per cent chance of failure, in which case they will lose all their money. The alternative is to place the money in a safe interest account, guaranteed to grow by $10,000 over the same period. Which should they choose?

Economic decision theory provides a rule for such risky choices called the *expected value* or EV rule. We can take our safe investment to be a sure thing, so we know that it will be worth $110,000 in five years' time. How do we value the risky choice? The theory says that we multiply the probability of each outcome by its value and add them together. If the business fails, we get 0.3

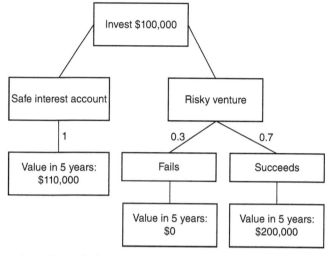

**8. Example of a decision tree.**

times 0 which equals 0. If it succeeds, we get 0.7 times \$200,000
which equals \$140,000. So the *expected value* of this choice is
\$140,000 which is evidently higher than the \$110,000 returned
from the interest account. On this basis the 'rational' choice is the
risky investment. Of course, it is not really as simple as that when
you consider the context. An investment bank might take this
choice because they have assets of billions and make a large number
of such risky investments. They can afford to lose some because
they will make big profits on others. But what if the \$100,000 is
the life savings of an individual planning to retire in five years?
Would it be rational for them to take a 30 per cent risk of losing
everything they have?

Two classic problems for the EV rule are insurance buying and
gambling. People do both even though they have expected losses.
Does this make them irrational? In the case of insurance, we can
consider an alternative decision rule: choose the option with the
*best security level*. That is the choice with the least worst outcome.

On that basis, it is rational to insure your house against fire because you could lose everything if it burns down. We can also factor in non-economic considerations, such as peace of mind. But it is still rational for the insurance companies to sell you insurance because the EV rule works in their favour: they will make profits. The difference is that they underwrite many policies and so have a large sample of cases, whereas the individual house owner has only one. It is similar to the investment decision shown in Figure 8. What looks like a good investment for a bank, seems like a reckless gamble for the life savings of an individual. The EV rule seems to work much better where there are many similar cases than when there is just one.

My intuition on this seems to be shared by most people. Suppose I gave you this choice:

A   I flip a coin. If it lands heads I will give you $200; if it lands tails you give me $100.

Research shows that most student participants will refuse such an offer, even though it gives them an expected gain of $50. Presumably, the reason is that they focus on the worst outcome and cannot afford to lose $100. Now consider this prospect:

B   I flip a coin 100 times. Each time it lands heads I will give you $200; each time it lands tails you give me $100.

Most people will accept B, even though each spin of the coin has the same expected value as A. Some psychologists and economists have described the preference for B over A as irrational, because it violates the expected value rule. But B is more like the case of the investment bank or the insurance company. The chance of losing money over 100 spins of the coin combined is very low.

The case of gambling is really problematic for decision theory. In Western societies, the majority of people gamble to some extent and a staggering 1–2 per cent are pathological gamblers. Much of this gambling is on games of chance, such as roulette, where expected losses are guaranteed (roulette wheels have one or two zeroes on them). Several million people fly into Las Vegas *every month* for the purpose of giving their money to the casinos. Betting on horse racing and all kinds of sporting events is widespread, even in the USA where it is mostly illegal. Like the casinos, the bookmakers set the odds in their favour and make good profits, so the gambler can again expect to lose money on a regular basis. They certainly do not have an expected gain like the investor in the risky company described earlier. Neither the EV rule nor the security level rule would endorse this behaviour. So why does it happen?

Economic decision theorists have tried to develop the EV rule by taking into account both subjective probabilities and the subject value of outcomes, termed *utility*. For example, if you are rich, the utility of a given amount of money may be smaller than if you are poor. A rich person might well take gamble A, because unlike the student participants they can easily afford to lose $100. Also, if probabilities are allowed to be subjective then this can explain some deviations from expected value. For example, if a gambler overestimates their probability of winning the national lottery, then buying a ticket may have a subjective expected gain for them. Then there are utilities for non-financial aspects such as the pleasure of gambling. A friend of mine who likes to go to horse race meetings once told me that he budgeted a few hundred pounds for gambling losses per year which was well worth the pleasure he got from attending meetings and backing horses. When I still tried to suggest his gambling was irrational, he asked me how much I spend per year on playing golf. Needless to say, it was a lot more!

There is no Nobel Prize for psychology, but occasionally a psychologist wins the economics prize. This last happened in 2002, where the recipient was Daniel Kahneman, in part for his work on prospect theory, in collaboration with Amos Tversky (who was not eligible for the prize, as he was by then deceased). Their work focussed on financial decisions and provided an alternative account to traditional economic theory. They included a number of simple psychological experiments showing that people would prefer one choice to another, even though they had the same expected value. One finding was the *certainty effect*. People have a strong preference for taking a sure thing over a risky prospect, as in the example shown in Figure 8. People's attitude to risk also seems to reflect the size of the probabilities concerned. Consider this choice:

Would you prefer a 0.45 chance of winning $6,000 or a 0.90 chance of winning $3,000?

Most people prefer the latter, the higher chance of winning money. Note that the expected value of the two options is the same. Now consider this choice:

Would you prefer a 0.001 chance of winning $6,000 or a 0.002 chance of winning $3,000?

In this case most people prefer the first option: the lower chance to win a larger amount, which seems inconsistent with the choice they make on the first problem. When winning is probable, they prefer the better chance. When it is a long shot, however, they prefer the greater reward. This may explain why people bet on national lotteries with large prizes but very low chances of winning.

Tversky and Kahneman also showed that the subjective value, or utility, that people have for money works differently for losses and gains. For example, consider this choice:

Would you prefer a 0.8 chance of winning $4,000 or have $3,000 for sure?

Most people here take the $3,000 even though the expected value of the risky prospect is a little higher, in line with the certainty effect. But now consider this choice:

> Would you prefer a 0.8 chance of losing $4,000 or to lose $3,000 for sure?

Now the pattern of choices flips over. Most people prefer to take the gamble of losing $4,000 rather than losing $3,000 for sure.

If this was the whole story then people would not buy insurance, in which they take the sure loss of premium rather than risk losing their house. But Kahneman and Tversky also showed that people overweight probabilities of events which are very low. It is very unlikely that our house will burn down but we still insure against it. It is also very unlikely that we will win the national lottery, but we still buy a ticket.

## Cognitive biases in decision making

In this section, I move away from the traditional economic approach to decision making and look instead at some of the psychological factors that influence our choices, not necessarily involving money at all. I have used the term 'bias' in labelling this section, but I will defer discussion for the time being of whether such biases make people irrational. The phenomena discussed are termed biases because they show that factors which appear to be irrelevant to the actual merit of the choices may affect our decision making.

When we give someone a decision to make, we can get a different answer according to how we ask the question, a phenomenon known as *framing*. The original work on this was again done by Kahneman and Tversky, some published in their papers on prospect theory and some separately. Here is one of their classic problems.

Imagine that the USA is preparing for the outbreak of an unusual Asian disease, which is expected to kill 600 people. Two alternative programmes to combat the disease have been proposed. Assume that exact scientific estimates of the consequences of following the programme are as follows:

> If programme A is adopted, 200 people will be saved.
>
> If programme B is adopted, there is a one-third probability that 600 people will be saved and a two-thirds probability that no people will be saved.

Most people (72 per cent) preferred programme A, although programme B also expects (in the mathematical sense) to save 200 people and could save all 600. This seems like another example of the certainty effect.

The question can be reframed, however, with different results when presented to a separate group of participants:

> If programme C is adopted, 400 people will die.
>
> If programme D is adopted, there is a one-third probability that nobody will die and a two-thirds probability that 600 people will die.

Now it was found that most people (78 per cent) preferred D to C. However, it is evident that A is logically equivalent to C, and that B is logically equivalent to D. So when the problem is framed in terms of the number of people dying rather than living, choices reverse with the risky option preferred. Kahneman and Tversky had already shown that the certainty effect reverses for losses. What is remarkable about this experiment, however, is that people will give completely opposite answers when the framing of the problem makes them think about positive or negative outcomes, without changing the logic of the choice in any way.

There is some cultural recognition that the framing of questions can affect decisions. This is particularly important when big questions are decided by referenda. In 2014, people living in Scotland were given a vote on Scottish independence from the UK, but the question to be asked was much debated. The original suggestion of 'Do you agree that Scotland should be an independent country?' was later altered to simply 'Should Scotland be an independent country?' in case the phrase 'Do you agree' somehow cued a 'Yes' answer. In the subsequent 2016 referendum on the UK leaving the European Union the question was again much debated. In the end 'Yes' and 'No' were avoided, with a choice between 'Remain' and 'Leave' presented. This was probably a good choice, as there may well be a preference for 'Yes' over 'No', whatever the question.

For some reason, people feel more responsible for actions than inactions and as a result can do harm by their failure to act, a phenomenon known as *omission bias*. The classical way of demonstrating this involves the vaccination problem. Participants are told that a disease kills 10 out of 1,000 children but that inoculation may kill between 0 and 9. They are asked what level of risk they would tolerate in order to administer the inoculation. Decision theory says that this should be set to 9 as there will still be a net saving of one life. However, research shows that only a small minority are willing to inoculate with this level of risk, with a larger number of participants tolerating no risk at all. This is classified as a cognitive bias because decision theory considers only the relative benefit of each outcome. The problem here might seem to be that people feel responsible for any deaths caused by a positive action (inoculation) but not for those caused by inaction (failure to inoculate). However, an alternative explanation has been offered: people more readily build causal mental models directly linking positive actions to effects. We can relate this to the positivity biases discussed in Chapter 2.

A very curious effect was reported by Eldar Shafir and colleagues in their studies of decision making. In one example, participants are told that they are a judge deciding to which parent of a child they should award custody. Attributes of the parents are given as follows:

Parent A Average income, average health, average working hours, reasonable rapport with child, relatively stable social life.

Parent B Above-average income, very close relationship with child, extremely active social life, lots of work-related travel, minor health problems.

When asked to whom they would award custody, 64 per cent said Parent B. A second group was asked to whom they would *deny* custody. Again Parent B was the more popular choice (55 per cent). But how can this be? To deny custody to B is to award it to A! The authors propose a psychological explanation, however. They suggest that in the Award group, people look for reasons to award custody and find some in the B list, e.g. good income and close relationship. In the Deny group they look for reasons to deny custody and again find some on the B list, e.g. active social life and work-related travel. By contrast, A is average on everything.

Clearly the finding seems irrational in terms of decision theory even if we can give it a psychological explanation. It can be seen as another kind of framing effect—asking the same question in a different way gets a different answer. It is also related to what has been described as *focussing bias* in decision making. It appears that we may be cued to think selectively about the available information when making decisions, which biases the outcome.

Also discussed by Shafir and colleagues is the *disjunction effect*. Again, this is best illustrated with an example problem. Participants are told that they face a tough qualifying examination, and if they fail they will have to retake it after the Christmas holidays. They also have the opportunity to buy an attractive vacation package in Hawaii for the Christmas period. One group were told they had passed the examination and the majority opted to book the vacation. Another group were told that they had failed, but again the majority opted to book the package. A third group were told they did not yet know if they had passed or failed. In this case, an astonishing 61 per cent were willing to pay a non-refundable $5 fee to defer a decision until the result of the examination was known. Why waste the charge for deferral when you would book the package on either result?

There are many demonstrations of the disjunction effect, which is of great psychological interest. It appears to be illogical. If you prefer A to B when C is true and also prefer A to B when C is false, then you must prefer A to B regardless of C. So why do people defer a decision? Shafir et al. suggest that people have different reasons for the two choices. We can again look at this in terms of causal mental models. One is:

Pass the examination → want to celebrate → book vacation

Another is

Fail the examination → need to cheer oneself up → book vacation

People do not seem to like holding two or more possible models in mind at the same time. I have suggested in one of my books that this is a general feature of hypothetical thinking, which I call the *singularity principle*. The disjunction effect appears to operate with stock markets, which are notoriously averse to uncertainty. For example, stocks often fall prior to a general election and then rise again, whatever the result.

Imagining future events is a type of hypothetical thinking which is key to rational decision making. However, a number of cognitive biases have been demonstrated relating to our ability to forecast or imagine the future. For example, human judgement has been shown to be chronically *overconfident*, so that, for example, we are less able to forecast future events, such as the outcome of sporting encounters, than we believe ourselves to be. (This may be a factor in the popularity of gambling on such events.) Overconfidence is a more general effect, however. For example, you can ask people to choose one of two meanings for unusual words and assign a probability that they are correct. Generally, the more confident they are, the more likely they are to be right, but the actual level of this confidence is too high. We can show this by checking all items for a given level of confidence and seeing how many were answered correctly. We may discover, for example, that on items where people say they are 80 per cent confident, they only get 70 per cent right. Expert groups are usually overconfident as well, unless they get very accurate feedback on repeated judgements, as in the case of weather forecasters.

Another bias in forecasting the future is known as the *planning fallacy*. When asked to predict how long a task will take, most people underestimate the time required. This is a curious effect because people seem to go about the task in the wrong way, even when they have relevant experience. Suppose I ask a colleague how long it will take her to write up a research paper for submission to a journal. What she could do is to recall her experience of writing similar papers in the past and how long they took and use this to estimate the time for the new one. This should be quite accurate. What people seem to do instead, however, is to run a mental simulation of the task. They imagine the different aspects they will need to complete but in an idealized manner. My colleague, for example, will assume that everything goes to plan and forget all the problems that held her up in various ways in the past and that will almost certainly happen again!

Routine decisions—such as whether to accept a cup of tea or coffee—can be made by habit and past experience. But some decisions are both important and do seem to require some mental simulation of the future. An example would be whether to accept a new job which is a promotion but requires you to uproot your family and move to a new location. There are many complexities to deal with. For example, people will try to find out what they can about the new world in which they would live but a lot would be left to guesswork. We can only imagine so much and there is scope also for focussing biases. For example, we may focus on imagining how happy we would be in the new job and not enough on what we would be leaving behind. Or we may focus on the job and not enough on the consequences for personal and family life. In the end we may give up on rational attempts to analyse such a difficult decision and rely on 'gut feelings'. I will discuss the role of such intuitions in decision making in Chapter 7.

## Probability judgement: heuristics and biases

The theory of rational decision making requires that we assign probabilities to events in order to devise a decision tree of the kind shown in Figure 8. Clearly, our ability to make effective decisions under risk requires us to estimate these probabilities with some accuracy. But how do we make such judgements, and are these also subject to cognitive biases? A consensual view in the 1960s was that people were pretty good intuitive statisticians. This idea was quite simply blown apart by a series of studies that commenced in the 1970s and which have strongly influenced the field to the present day. This is the other work for which Daniel Kahneman received a Nobel Prize, also in collaboration with the late Amos Tversky. They initiated what has become known as the *heuristics and biases* research programme. Vast amounts of research have followed, involving many different authors.

What Kahneman and Tversky did was to propose that we judge probabilities by applying certain heuristics, but that these can lead to cognitive biases. As discussed in Chapter 2, a heuristic is a short-cut method to solving a problem that may work quickly but may also fail. As an example, consider the *availability heuristic* proposed by Kahneman and Tversky. This is the proposal that we judge the probability of events by the examples that we can call to mind. Suppose that someone asks me how many goals, on average, are scored by Arsenal football club in each match. I am a big Arsenal fan and follow most of their games on television or radio, always checking the results of those I miss. So I could attempt to answer this by calling to mind different games and estimating the average number of goals. I might be quite good at this but there could still be biases due to the way human memory works. For example, I might remember more of their better games and so overestimate the number of goals. Or I might remember more of their recent games and hence be biased by a particularly good or poor run of form.

Kahneman and Tversky demonstrated many such biases resulting from the availability heuristic. For example, if you ask people if there are more English words with the letter 'k' in the first or third position, most people say the first even though there are actually twice as many words with a k in the third position. The reason, it seems, is that it is much easier to retrieve words from memory by their initial letter and hence draw examples to mind. However, they also proposed other heuristics which apply in different circumstances, the most important of which is *representativeness*. This can be illustrated with their famous Linda problem. Participants are told that Linda is thirty-one years old, single, outspoken, and very bright. She majored in philosophy and was deeply concerned with issues of social justice and discrimination, and also participated in anti-nuclear demonstrations.

Participants are then asked to rate the likelihood of several statements including the following:

1. Linda is a bank teller
2. Linda is a feminist
3. Linda is a bank teller and a feminist

The stereotype elicited by the description of Linda suggests she is much more likely to be a feminist than a bank teller, so people rate 2 as more likely than 1. The interesting result is that they also rate 3 as more likely than 1, which is illogical. This is termed the *conjunction fallacy*. The point is that the probability of two events A and B can never be more likely than the probability of either one of them. There has been much research on this problem, and much debate about the cause of the conjunction fallacy. The original account was that 3 is more representative of the image you have of Linda than 1. It is easier to imagine her being a bank teller if she is also a feminist. But of course, since only some bank tellers are feminists, it must be less likely overall.

In Chapter 5, I will discuss some further work on how people reason with probabilities. I should also mention that there have been many critics of the heuristics and biases programme, and especially the view that this work shows people to be irrational. I will cover this debate in Chapter 6, along with an alternative programme of work led by one of these critics, Gerd Gigerenzer, who has proposed that use of heuristics can lead instead to rational and appropriate decision making.

## Conclusions

By necessity, this chapter provides an introduction to human decision making that is very short indeed. There is a theory of rational decision making that comes largely from economics but has had much influence in psychology. This theory requires that people project future consequences of their choices, estimating probabilities and values and generally choosing the options with the best (mathematically) expected value. Against this we have a wealth of psychological evidence that both decision making and probability judgement are subject to a whole host of cognitive biases. This conflict is the main cause of the debate about human rationality that we will look at in Chapter 6. The debate also reflects evidence that our reasoning fails to meet the required normative standards, which I discuss in Chapter 5.

# Chapter 5
# **Reasoning**

We can come to know things directly or by reasoning. For example, suppose I know Mary and her daughter Sue. One day, I meet Mary and she introduces me to her brother Paul. The next time I see Sue, I might ask her about her uncle Paul. But no one actually told me that Paul was her uncle—I *inferred* it. Like most people, I have learned a general rule: the brother of a parent is the uncle of their children. In this case I applied the rule, probably without any conscious reflection, to infer that Paul is Sue's uncle (and similarly, that she is his niece). Consider how difficult it would be if we could not make inferences of this kind. We would have to store all family relations separately for every individual we know, which would be most inefficient. Sometimes we need to reason with explicit rules that are much less familiar than this, for example to work out how much tax we owe the government at the end of the year. Knowing which rules to apply and how to calculate their effects can be difficult in such cases and we might decide to employ a professional to do it for us.

In this chapter I consider deductive reasoning, where we can draw conclusions from assumptions which necessarily follow, and also statistical inference, in which we infer probabilities from other probabilities. These two fields of psychological study have a lot in common. First, both present problems where you are given some information and asked to draw an inference.

Second, each has what is called a *normative theory*, a set of rules which tells us which conclusions are right and which are wrong. In the case of deductive reasoning the normative theory is logic, and in the case of statistical inference it is probability theory. Third, each field shows that many of the answers given by individuals are wrong by these norms, fuelling a debate about human rationality.

## Deductive reasoning

Logic is a core topic in philosophy and has been so since the time of Aristotle. Logical reasoning involves the deduction of conclusions from assumptions, usually known as the *premises* of the argument. For example, if I tell you that all psychologists are friendly and that Sarah is a psychologist, you must conclude that Sarah is friendly. Note that you don't actually have to believe this conclusion to be true. If the premises are *assumed* to be true then the conclusion follows because this argument is valid in logic. By definition, a valid argument is one that ensures that a conclusion is true, provided that the premises are true. Of course, some arguments are fallacies. So if I tell you that all psychologists are friendly and that Sarah is friendly, it would be a fallacy to conclude that she is a psychologist. This conclusion could very well be false, even when the premises are true.

When we say that someone is reasoning logically, we mean that they are making valid arguments and avoiding fallacies. This kind of reasoning was long regarded as the key definition of rational thinking. For this reason, a large field of psychological study developed in which people are given reasoning problems to solve, which are then assessed against some standard kind of logic. The earliest such studies were reported in the 1920s and 1930s and the field expanded rapidly from the 1960s onwards. The most common method is to give people the premises of an argument, together with a potential conclusion, and ask them whether the conclusion follows. For example, they might be shown the following argument which applies to a card which has a letter on one side and a number on the other:

*Premises*
If there is a B on the card then there is a 6 on the card
There is a B on the card

*Conclusion*
Therefore, there is a 6 on the card

Almost everyone will agree here that the conclusion follows. This is a very simple and valid logical inference known as *modus ponens*. The general convention in studying deduction is that participants are not given any instruction in logic, as the purpose is to test whether they are inherently logical. However, it is normal to tell people to assume the premises are true and only endorse a conclusion which *necessarily* follows. This instruction broadly indicates what a valid argument is, and also implies that what they actually believe is irrelevant.

While *modus ponens* may be very easy, other similar-looking inferences are not. For example:

*Premises*
If there is a B on the card then there is a 6 on the card
There is not a 6 on the card

*Conclusion*
Therefore, there is not a B on the card

This inference, called *modus tollens*, is also logically valid, but only about two-thirds of participants, typically university students, will say that the conclusion necessarily follows. Now consider this argument:

*Premises*
If there is a B on the card then there is a 6 on the card
There is a 6 on the card

*Conclusion*
Therefore, there is a B on the card

Many students, sometimes a majority, will say that this conclusion necessarily follows, even though it does not. This is a fallacy, similar to the one about Sarah being a psychologist given earlier. In that case, with real life terms, the fallacy was obvious. Here, with letters and numbers, it is much less so, although the rule does not require a B to be on the back of a 6. Despite many years of research on such problems, we still do not really understand why they are so difficult for participants to solve. However, we do know that those with higher IQs generally get more of them right.

The plot thickens if we use conditional statements, of the form 'if…then…', with more realistic content. Now people are influenced by whether or not they believe the statement. Suppose we give the following *modus ponens* argument:

If nurses' pay is increased then recruitment to the profession will fall
Nurses' pay is increased
Therefore, recruitment to the profession will fall

In this case, most people would not believe the conditional statement to be true, as increasing pay ought, if anything, to increase recruitment. If university students are given a problem like this, many will refuse to endorse the conclusion. It appears that their actual beliefs block the inference. However, if we give strong logical reasoning instructions we find that those of higher IQ will mostly restore *modus ponens*, and say that the conclusion does follow after all. But participants of lower ability still mostly stick with what they believe, rather than adhere to logic.

We can also suppress *modus ponens* by giving people additional information which does not affect the logic of the inference. Suppose we give the following problem:

If Ruth meets her friend, she will go to the theatre
Ruth meets her friend
What follows?

Most people will naturally say that Ruth will go to the theatre. For a different group, we add a sentence:

If Ruth meets her friend, she will go to the theatre
If Ruth has enough money, she will go to the theatre
Ruth meets her friend
What follows?

Now many people will block the *modus ponens* inference and say that nothing follows. Obviously what happens here is that people start to think that if Ruth does not have enough money then she cannot go to the theatre, even if she meets her friend. But technically this is illogical. If the first and third statements are true, as people are instructed, then *modus ponens* still applies.

These findings, and many similar ones, tell us something very interesting. It appears that belief-based reasoning is the norm with human beings, regardless of ability. Some people can, when required, set aside their beliefs and reason in an abstract logical manner. We know this must be true, because people can become, for example, highly skilled mathematicians. But such logical reasoning is not as normal and natural as many philosophers and psychologists had at one time assumed. It seems to require a combination of high IQ and a good deal of conscious effort to achieve. It may also require extensive training, as in the case of mathematics.

## Syllogistic reasoning and belief bias

The oldest system of formal logic was developed by Aristotle and is known as a categorical syllogism. Syllogisms relate three terms in two premises. The first premise links A to B and the second B to C. The conclusion, which may or may not follow, links A to C. They can be presented in various forms. Here is an easy one:

All A are B
All B are C
Therefore, all A are C

This syllogism is valid and everyone can see that—as easy as *modus ponens*. But suppose it is worded as follows:

All A are B
All C are B
Therefore, all C are A

This argument is not valid, but many university students nevertheless say that it is. I can easily convince you they are wrong by putting in some realistic terms for A, B, and C:

All dogs are animals
All cats are animals
Therefore, all cats are dogs

Needless to say, no one would agree that this is a valid argument but its form is exactly the same as the A, B, C version. It is the form that defines validity, not the content. This shows again how difficult most people find it to reason in an abstract logical manner. Using our beliefs does not necessarily improve our reasoning, however. In fact, it can be a major source of bias. Here is quite a tricky syllogism in abstract form. Try to decide whether or not it is logically valid:

No A are B
Some C are B
Therefore, some A are not C

Difficult, is it not? Here is a version with the same form but with realistic terms:

No addictive things are inexpensive
Some cigarettes are inexpensive
Therefore, some addictive things are not cigarettes

In one frequently cited study, 71 per cent of university students tested said that this was a valid argument. They were also given the following syllogism to evaluate:

No millionaires are hard workers
Some rich people are hard workers
Therefore, some millionaires are not rich people

In this case, only 10 per cent of the students tested said that the conclusion followed logically. But if you look closely, you can see that both of these realistic versions have exactly the same logical form. All we have done is substitute different realistic terms for A, B, and C. In logic, the actual meaning of the three terms is irrelevant. This form of syllogism is not, in fact, a valid argument. (However, if the conclusion were 'Some C are not A', it would follow.) So why do so many people mistakenly say that the conclusion 'some addictive things are not cigarettes' follows, but correctly reject the conclusion 'some millionaires are not rich people'? The answer has been established beyond any reasonable doubt by many psychological experiments. The first conclusion is *believable* and the second *unbelievable*. Even with clear logical reasoning instructions, people are strongly inclined to say that believable conclusions follow and unbelievable ones do not. This is known as the *belief bias* effect.

The paper which established the nature of belief bias (first authored by myself) was also a foundation for the modern dual-process theory of reasoning. We argued that there was conflict between an unconscious or Type 1 belief bias and a conscious or Type 2 attempt to reason logically as instructed. Using protocol analysis, we showed that logical responses were more often associated with attention to the premises of the argument and belief-based processes more often with a focus on the conclusion. We also showed that when belief and logic were in conflict, the same participant might follow a Type 1 or Type 2 route on different occasions. For this reason, belief bias is often referred to (and debated) as a paradigm case for the dual-process theory.

## Mental model theory

One of the most influential theories in the psychology of reasoning is the mental model theory, proposed and developed over many years by Phil Johnson-Laird and his collaborators. In this theory, mental models represent possible states of affairs which may be true or false in the real world. People reason by constructing models of the premises of an argument that represent possibilities. Any statement which is true in all the possibilities they consider can be drawn as a valid conclusion. However, people make mistakes because these models are often incomplete and overlook possibilities. This can happen because people have a limited capacity to think about multiple models and also because they focus on what is true rather than what is false.

Model theory has an explanation for the belief bias effect. Consider the same syllogism I have been discussing as an example. People should construct mental models equivalent to the two situations shown in Figure 9, but syllogisms consistent with more than one model are always more difficult. The first model shown in Figure 9 is true for both the premises and conclusion. If there were no alternative, the syllogism would be valid. But in Model 2, we see that the premises can be true and the conclusion false. Model 2 provides a *counterexample*, to show that the inference is invalid. The mental model account of belief bias was originally that people fail to look for counterexamples when they believe the conclusion to be true, so they consider only Model 1. There is also evidence that people may try from the start to construct a model which supports a believable conclusion or refutes an unbelievable

Model 1

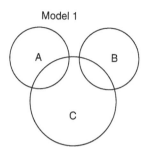

Model 2

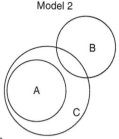

Some A are not C?

A = addictive things
B = inexpensive things
C = cigarettes

A = millionaires
B = hard workers
C = rich people

**9. Alternative models for the same syllogism.**

one. Either way, this is an example of *motivated reasoning*, for which there is much evidence in social psychology.

Johnson-Laird and his colleagues also discovered an interesting set of *illusory inferences*, where people draw the opposite conclusion to that which follows logically. Consider this problem. Only one of these two conditional statements is true:

(1)   If there is a King in the hand then there is an Ace in the hand

or else

(2)   If there is a Queen in the hand then there is an Ace in the hand

Most people will conclude that there is an Ace in the hand. Indeed Johnson-Laird made this inference himself, until his computer program told him it was a fallacy. He even searched for a bug in the program! According to the theory, people imagine a King with an Ace if (1) is true, and a Queen with an Ace if (2) is true, and so an Ace is always present. But they forget that one of the statements must be *false*, which is the key to

72

finding the correct answer. If (1) is false, then there must be a King and not an Ace. If (2) is false, there must be a Queen and not an Ace. Either way, there is not an Ace! A very powerful illusion indeed.

Mental model theory holds that people have a method of reasoning which is sound in principle, but often flawed in practice. However, there is a rival theory which says that people reason by access to a mental logic: a set of rules for reasoning built into the mind. There has been a long argument as to whether people reason using models or rules. This has never been clearly resolved, although it is fair to say that the model theory is more popular and has inspired many more research papers.

## Reasoning with probabilities

In Chapter 4, I discussed the conjunction fallacy (Linda problem), in which people assign probabilities to events in an apparently illogical manner. There is actually a mass of evidence that our intuitions about probability and our ability to draw correct inferences from them are quite weak. We can test people's ability to reason with probabilities in a similar way that we run experiments on deductive reasoning. That is, we can give some information and ask people to draw an inference from it. As an example, consider the following medical diagnosis problem:

Version A:  If a test to detect a disease whose prevalence is 1/1,000 has a false positive rate of 5 per cent, what is the chance that a person found to have a positive result actually has the disease, assuming you know nothing about the person's symptoms and signs?

This version of the problem was presented to medical students and junior doctors, with alarming results. The most commonly given answer was 95 per cent whereas the correct answer is approximately 2 per cent! It was later shown that the problem is much easier to understand if framed in terms of frequencies, as the next version shows:

Version B:   1 out of every 1,000 Americans has disease X. A test has been developed to detect when a person has disease X. Every time the test is given to a person who has the disease, the test comes out positive (i.e. the 'true positive rate' is 100 per cent). But sometimes, the test also comes out positive when it is given to a person who is completely healthy. Specifically, out of every 1,000 people who are perfectly healthy, fifty of them test positive (the 'false positive rate' is 5 per cent).

With Version B, when asked how many of the positive testers have the disease, one study showed that 56 per cent of participants gave the correct answer of 2 per cent. This is much better, but I would still like *all* my doctors to know how to interpret a diagnostic test!

Here is an intuitive explanation of the correct answer. Imagine we have 1,000 people of whom one has the disease. The other 999 will yield approximately fifty positive results, all of which are false. So of those testing positive, only around 1/50 can actually have the disease (see Figure 10). And yet on Version A,

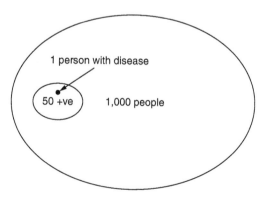

**10. Representation of the medical diagnosis problem.**

participants with medical training were inferring that this number was actually 95 per cent! The false positive rate of 5 per cent is the probability of a positive result given a healthy participant. As such, 95 per cent is the probability of a negative result given a healthy participant which, of course, is not the answer to the question given. There is clearly some very shallow reasoning going on here. Perhaps people just assume that the test is right 95 per cent of the time, regardless of who is being tested.

Why is Version B easier? This version expresses the probabilities using frequency information. For example, we tell participants that fifty out of 1,000 healthy people test positive rather than simply saying that the false positive rate is 5 per cent. Some authors have argued that we evolved to deal with frequency information in the environment, while the concept of probability is a very late invention of human scholars. However, the evolutionary account of the frequency effect has been strongly contested and a vigorous debate ensued.

The normative theory for this problem is Bayes' theorem, an important proof within probability theory. For the technically minded, a formal definition of Bayes' theorem is provided in the Appendix, along with a proof of the 2 per cent solution for the medical diagnosis problem. What the theorem captures is the idea that our belief in hypotheses after examining some evidence should be determined both by our prior belief in them and the evidence examined. Belief always changes in the direction of the evidence but by variable amounts. Suppose a juror during a trial is currently thinking that a defendant is probably guilty when some evidence supporting her innocence is presented. If the prior belief of guilt was very strong and the evidence weak it might not change their verdict. But if they were not fully convinced of guilt or the evidence was strong, then it could be enough to create reasonable doubt. This is known as Bayesian reasoning.

In laboratory tasks, 'prior belief' is usually established through the presentation of base rate information and it appears that Bayesian reasoning is biased. It has been known for some time that when people try to solve such problems they pay insufficient attention to the base rate. One famous demonstration of this, first presented by Tversky and Kahneman, is known as the cabs problem. Participants are told that two cab companies run in a city: the Blue cab company, which has 85 per cent of the city's cabs, and the Green cab company, which has 15 per cent. A cab is involved in a hit and run accident and a witness later identified the cab as a Green one. Under tests, the witness was shown to be able to identify the colour of a cab correctly about 80 per cent of the time under similar viewing conditions, but would confuse it with the other colour about 20 per cent of the time. The participants are then asked whether it is more likely that the cab is, in fact, a Green or Blue one. Most say Green, although the correct answer is, in fact, Blue.

The correct answer can be proven with Bayes' theorem, presented in the Appendix, but a more intuitive proof again uses frequencies. Imagine there are 100 cabs in the city of which 85 are blue and 15 green. Of the 85 blue ones, 20 per cent would be mistakenly identified as green, that is 17 of them. Of the 15 green ones, 80 per cent would be correctly identified as green, that is 12. So the odds are 17:12 in favour of blue. This is illustrated visually in Figure 11.

Research on problems like these shows that people pay insufficient attention to base rate information. But psychological manipulations can change this. One is the use of frequency formats, as we have already seen. Another is the use of framing that elicits causal mental models. If the cabs problem is presented with the following variant, a dramatically different result ensues. In this version you tell people that there are an

**15 Green Cabs**       **85 Blue Cabs**

12 Identified as Green (80%)

17 Identified as Green (20%)

11. **Representation of the cabs problem.**

equal number of green and blue cabs in the city but that 85
per cent of the cabs *involved in accidents* are blue. The rest of
the problem is the same, as is the correct answer since 85 per
cent provides the relevant base rate for the problem. With this
framing, most people correctly say the cab is more likely to be
blue. Now that people can see a causal basis for the base rate
(the blue cab company employs dangerous drivers) they pay
more attention to this information.

The errors in statistical reasoning that research studies like these
reveal are clearly very important for real life decision making. It
is essential, for example, that doctors know how to make correct
Bayesian inferences when interpreting diagnostic tests and that
courts of law know how to interpret statistical evidence, as in
the case of DNA tests. In an argument known as the *prosecutor's
fallacy*, a lawyer may argue, solely on the basis of a positive DNA
test, that a defendant is guilty. The argument goes like this: only
one person in 100,000 would match the sample found at the
crime scene, therefore a person testing positive is 99.99 per cent
likely to be guilty. But this inference is a fallacy which actually
confuses two different probabilities. The probability of a positive

test given that you are innocent, has been turned into the probability of being innocent given that you have a positive test result. This conversion is invalid and base rates again have to be considered. In a city of a million people, ten would match the sample. So if someone is found by mass DNA testing with no other evidence against them, the chances of them being innocent are very much higher than the prosecutor is arguing.

## Bayesianism and the new paradigm psychology of reasoning

Bayesianism is more than just the application of Bayes' theorem. It is a philosophical and mathematical movement that is having increasing influence throughout cognitive psychology. Bayesians focus on belief, represented as *subjective* probabilities, ranging (like objective ones) between 0 and 1. Objective probabilities are usually defined by long-term frequencies. For example, on the latter view, if the probability of a coin landing heads is 0.5 this means that it would land heads 50 per cent of the time in a large series of tosses. But how do you determine the odds if you are going to bet on just one spin of a coin? On the subjective view, proposed by Bayesians, you can assign a subjective probability of 0.5 meaning that you have no better reason to believe that it will land heads than tails. This means that you can apply probability to one-time risky decisions of the kind which occur frequently in real life. When you choose a career or a marriage partner there are certainly risks to consider, but you don't get a long run of such choices for them to even out!

Bayes' theorem, together with subjective probability and utility (subjective value), and incorporating both probability theory and decision theory, has been developed into a mathematical and philosophical system. Beliefs defined as subjective probabilities can be revised as new evidence is encountered, by application of Bayes' theorem. Bayesianism also provides an alternative philosophy of science to the logical method of Karl Popper, discussed in Chapter 2. Bayesians do not seek absolute confirmation or refutation but rather revise their beliefs continually in the face of evidence. Popper thought of probability as objective and hence could not assign a probability to a scientific theory which is like a single event. You cannot, for example, sensibly ask how often Darwin's principle of natural selection would be correct in a long run of opportunities. But you can assign a degree of belief to it, expressed as a subjective probability.

When we first encounter a theory, we may find it plausible, implausible, or be indifferent to it, assigning beliefs of say 0.8, 0.2 or 0.5 respectively. However, if the evidence is strong and consistent enough, the theory will eventually be believed no matter how sceptical the original opinion. There are many examples of this in the history of science. Take the case of the geocentric theory, in which the Sun is believed to revolve around the Earth, and which dominated science for some 1,500 years after its proposal by Aristotle and Ptolemy. It was not until the 17th century that it was challenged by Copernicus and Kepler who initially met with great cultural and religious resistance. But the evidence for the heliocentric theory eventually overwhelmed this unfavourable prior belief, so that one theory replaced the other. In general, the evidence suggests that real scientists appear to behave much more like Bayesians than Popperians.

Faced with the evidence of illogical reasoning in the study of deduction, psychologists could either declare people to be irrational (as some did, including Peter Wason) or else question the use of logic as the standard to judge them by. From the 1990s onwards, many researchers began to doubt the standard paradigm, not just because of implausibly high error levels but also due to the strong evidence that human reasoning appears to be inherently belief-based. In fact, a large number of researchers in the field no longer see traditional logic as the benchmark of good reasoning. One major and influential research programme has been led by Mike Oaksford and Nick Chater, who have been interpreting deductive reasoning as probabilistic since the early 1990s and clearly regard everyday reasoning as rational from a Bayesian perspective. This is part of what is known as the *new paradigm* psychology of reasoning, although other authors in this paradigm do not necessarily share their view that human reasoning is strictly Bayesian.

In the new paradigm, conditional statements are given a probabilistic interpretation. Instead of asking people if conditionals are true or false, we can ask them instead to judge the extent to which they believe them, by assigning a probability. In one study, conducted by David Over and colleagues, people were asked to assign a probability to statements conveying everyday causal relationships, such as:

If global warming increases then London will be flooded

In a separate task, the same participants were also asked to assign probabilities to the following events:

A  Global warming will increase and London will be flooded: 0.4
B  Global warming will increase and London will not be flooded: 0.2
C  Global warming will not increase and London will be flooded: 0.3
D  Global warming will not increase and London will not be flooded: 0.1

I include here an illustrative set of responses which must add up to 1. This task was repeated for many other causal conditional statements. It turned out that people were really only influenced by A and B in deciding whether they believed the conditional statement. In general their ratings implied the following:

| The probability that 'if global warming continues then London will be flooded' | = | The probability that 'London will be flooded given that global warming continues' |
|---|---|---|

That is, the rated probability of the conditional was very close to the rating of A divided by A + B. In the example given, they would rate the conditional statement as around 0.67 (0.4/0.6). What should the probability be according to standard logic? Traditionally, the conditional is considered true in all cases except B, so people should assign a probability of around 0.8, although hardly anyone does this. It seems they conduct a mental simulation in which they imagine the state of affairs in which global warming continues, and on this basis try to decide how likely it is that London will be flooded. Hence, they ignore their beliefs about cases where global warming does not continue. This finding confirms the views of contemporary philosophers, such as Dorothy Edgington, that the conditional statement of everyday language does not have the meaning normally given to it in logic textbooks. It is also of fundamental importance for the new paradigm psychology of reasoning.

For many years it seemed that logical reasoning was a quite separate matter from reasoning with probabilities. Over time it became clear that abstract, logical reasoning is not something that ordinary people can do at all well without training and that the natural mode of reasoning is belief-based. People also lack the ability to reason correctly with probabilities presented in formal problems, again without special training. There is, however, increasing evidence that people are at least broadly Bayesian, in that they hold beliefs with varying degrees of subjective probability and update them as they encounter new evidence. In the new paradigm psychology of reasoning, logic is no longer regarded as the clear standard for rational reasoning. Instead, the interest is in how people make use of their existing beliefs when they reason with new evidence. How they do this and the extent to which they are acting like 'good' Bayesians is the subject of much debate.

# Chapter 6
# Are we rational?

Most of the topics covered in this book allow human thinking and reasoning to be compared with a 'normative' standard, a formal theory of right and wrong answers. The normative theories mostly applied are decision theory, probability theory, or logic. We have seen that people frequently make errors by these standards and have been shown to have many cognitive biases. Some psychologists and philosophers have wondered whether this means that human beings must be intrinsically irrational. This question is not as simple as it seems, however, and has been the subject of much fierce debate over the past thirty years and more.

There are a number of different ways of defining rationality. For example, philosophers distinguish between *instrumental rationality* (how we should behave) and *epistemic rationality* (what we should believe). We are instrumentally rational when we act so as to achieve our goals. If we did not achieve basic biological goals such as eating, drinking, and reproduction then our species would not survive. However, for human beings many goals are much more complex than these and can easily be in conflict with each other. For example, a short-term goal, such as enjoying a night drinking with friends, may conflict with a long-term career goal when there is an important examination to be taken in the morning. In such cases, deciding what behaviour is instrumentally rational is not straightforward.

In Chapter 1, I described the behaviourist movement which was dominant in psychology for the best part of fifty years. Behaviourists believed that studying animal learning would tell us much about human behaviour. The focus was entirely on instrumental rationality (e.g. how animals learn to obtain food) and mostly on basic goals. The behaviourist movement showed scant interest in the representation and processing of knowledge in the human mind. Philosophers, however, had long recognized its importance, discussing *epistemic rationality*. We are epistemically rational when we acquire true beliefs about the world around us. But we also need to be able to deduce the correct inferences from these beliefs. Hence, the psychology of reasoning is primarily concerned with studying epistemic rationality. Decision making, by contrast, is concerned with people making the correct choices to achieve their goals and appears to focus on instrumental rationality.

It is not really as simple as that, however, as many decisions are based on beliefs. For example, in the 2016 UK referendum on membership of the European Union, the polling evidence suggests that the following beliefs were critical:

(1)  If the UK leaves the European Union then the economy will suffer badly

(2)  If the UK leaves the European Union then it will regain control of borders and restrict immigration

There were other issues, of course, but these seem to have been the most influential arguments, with (1) the most important factor for those voting Remain and (2) the most important for those voting Leave. The proponents of the two campaigns focussed largely on trying to build belief in (1) or (2), depending on their position. To be instrumentally rational, people should consider *both* of these issues, and a number of others, as the decision affects them in multiple ways. However, people tend to focus on single issues in their decision making. Clearly, the voting is also only justified if their beliefs are *true* or at least highly probable. This shows that epistemic rationality is also required for instrumental rationality in decision making. In the referendum, it was very difficult for people to decide the truth of either (1) or (2), partly due to the complexity of the issues and partly due to the highly partisan and misleading campaigning on both sides—a good case, one might think, for not deciding complex and multifaceted issues by referendum.

Another useful concept, proposed by Herb Simon, is that of *bounded rationality*. People have limited capabilities and may not be able to follow strategies considered optimal by mathematicians. If I ask you to tell me the square root of 8,958,049 by mental arithmetic, you will doubtless fail to give the correct answer (2,993). But no one would judge you to be irrational as a result. The study of heuristics to reduce problem search spaces, discussed in Chapter 2, is in the bounded rationality tradition. Such methods enable us to solve at least some of the problems that are beyond computation by straightforward means. In the bounded rationality approach, people still strive to achieve their goals, but their rationality is limited by their cognitive ability.

A few other definitions of rationality are worth a mention. Some authors refer to *normative rationality*, meaning behaviour which complies with a normative theory, such as logic. Whether such behaviour is also instrumentally rational is one of the issues debated in the field. Some have made the case that these two concepts should be treated separately, but others have suggested that a normative theory is simply a formal description of what it is to be instrumentally rational. There are widely different views on the value of normative theories, as we shall see later. Another concept is *ecological rationality*, which refers to behaviour that is adapted to the environment; yet another is *evolutionary rationality*, which is behaviour that has evolved to achieve the goals of our genes. I will discuss examples of all of these in this chapter.

# The great rationality debate

In this book, we have seen many examples of cognitive biases. In deductive reasoning, people make frequent logical errors and are prone to matching and belief biases. In statistical reasoning, people appear to have little understanding of the importance of base rate statistics, sometimes leading them to draw highly inaccurate inferences. In decision making, people may give very different answers to the questions according to how the information is framed, may be highly overconfident in forecasts and judgements, and so on. In each of these cases there is a well-established normative theory—logic, probability theory, decision theory—which allows us to calculate the correct answers. If traditional philosophers were right in proposing these norms as measures of rational thought, then it appears that people are inherently *irrational*. However, a number of psychologists and philosophers have been reluctant to draw this conclusion, leading to major arguments in the academic journals. This is sometimes referred to as 'the great rationality debate'.

At the heart of this debate is what I like to call the *paradox of rationality*. Outside of the psychologist's laboratory, the human species is quite evidently highly intelligent and successful compared with any other animal. We have advanced knowledge of mathematics, science, and engineering, and uniquely among animals can design and build environments to suit ourselves. For example, animals that live in the Arctic have evolved and adapted to do so by very slow processes. Humans, by contrast, can design and construct warm clothing, heated buildings, snow ploughs, etc. in order quickly to inhabit such a hostile environment. We appear to be instrumentally rational and indeed highly intelligent in how we go about achieving our goals in difficult circumstances. So the paradox is this: if people are so smart, how is it that psychological experiments on reasoning and judgement make them look dumb?

The debate sparked into life for psychologists following the publication of a major paper by the philosopher Jonathan Cohen in 1981, who argued that such experiments could *not* demonstrate human irrationality. His arguments and those of similarly minded authors are of three main kinds, and have featured in the debate ever since. The first is that people appear to be in error because the experimenter has applied the wrong normative theory. For example, Wason's logical analysis of his selection task (Chapter 2) has been disputed, and others have argued that from the perspective of decision theory, the standard choices can be deemed quite rational. In fact, many of the problems studied by psychologists are ambiguous in this way, with rival normative theories disputing the right answers.

The second issue is whether the participant interprets the problem in the way the experimenter intended. Recall the Linda problem presented in Chapter 4. People are judged to be illogical because they say that the probability of Linda being a bank teller and a feminist is higher than that of her being a bank teller. But suppose that in the context of the experiment, they assume that 'Linda is a bank teller' means 'Linda is a bank teller who is *not* a feminist'. Now there is no conjunction fallacy and one can quite rationally judge this to be less likely than her being a bank teller who is a feminist.

Other authors have suggested that people may make apparent fallacies in deductive reasoning because they supplement the information given with prior knowledge. For example, suppose we ask someone to evaluate this inference:

> If carbon emissions are not curbed then global warming will continue.
>
> Supposing that global warming does continue, does it follow that carbon emissions have not been curbed?

If they answer yes, then we could count this as a logical error or a fallacy. It does not follow from the information given as global warming might continue for other reasons. But if the individual is not aware of other causes of global warming, or discounts them, then the conclusion *does* follow when this knowledge is added to the premise given. There are many experiments showing that people use their knowledge precisely in this way.

Many of the arguments about rationality revolve around people's use of their prior knowledge when attempting laboratory tasks. On the one hand, it seems rational in everyday life to use all relevant knowledge when reasoning and making decisions. On the other hand, doing so in experiments often means that people are ignoring the instructions they were given. For example, people often prefer believable conclusions in reasoning experiments even when they were explicitly told to base their reasoning only on the information presented. The evidence suggests that only people of higher general intelligence find it easy to ignore their beliefs in order to comply with the instructions. But we could say that these experiments are artificial and unrepresentative of the real world. That, in fact, was Cohen's third argument. He suggested that errors in such experiments do not imply irrationality in everyday life.

It is tempting, but hazardous, to assume that laboratory results do apply to real world situations. For example, many authors have assumed that Wason's 2-4-6 problem, discussed in Chapter 3, was an analogue of scientific hypothesis testing, suggesting that scientists may have a confirmation bias. But some authors who have examined this task closely have concluded that it is actually not representative of scientific reasoning, and that in any case it does not necessarily show a bias to confirm hypotheses. Similar problems have arisen with the use of the Wason selection task. During the 1980s and 1990s there was a great deal of interest in the selection task, and a number of major papers were written about it by people who did not normally study human reasoning. I remember being concerned about it at the time because I was aware that very little reasoning underlies the card choices that most people make. With the exception of a small number of participants with very high IQs, choices are mostly determined by matching bias or prior beliefs. This does not undermine the psychological interest the task provides, but it does make it a poor choice if you want to draw general conclusions about people's reasoning ability.

Cohen's paper left a lasting impression on the psychology of thinking. By no means all psychologists see their work on thinking and reasoning as demonstrating irrationality, but most do feel obliged now to take some position on the topic. Some maintain that cognitive biases are real and a problem in everyday life. Such authors may propose training and education to improve human reasoning. However, a number of authors continue to argue, like Cohen, that people only appear to be irrational because the wrong norm is applied or the experiment is artificial or misleading in some way. Some assume that human rationality is a given. They argue that by a combination of evolution and learning, human behaviour *must* be well adapted to its environment and that we must therefore be capable of accurate and appropriate reasoning. Hence our theories of what people should do must be determined by consideration of what they actually do. I look at this approach next.

## Rational analysis

Rational analysis is an approach advocated by the famous cognitive psychologist, John Anderson. In the psychology of reasoning and decision making, the best known authors to adopt rational analysis are Mike Oaksford and Nick Chater. They assume that human behaviour will be adapted to the environment. So when behaviour conflicts with a standard normative theory of what people should do, there must be something wrong with the theory.

As Oaksford and Chater put it in their 2007 book: 'This viewpoint takes everyday rationality as fundamental, and dismisses the apparent mismatch between human reasoning and the formal principles of logic and probability theory as so much the worse for these formal theories.'

Rational analysis was one of the drivers for the new paradigm psychology of reasoning, discussed in Chapter 5. We know that people often reason illogically and therefore appear irrational by this standard. As a result, many researchers have agreed that we should move away from logic as the standard for human reasoning. Some take the view that we should focus more on describing what people do, rather than judging their behaviour as right or wrong. Others, however, want to define the new paradigm in terms of a new theory of good and bad reasoning, to replace logic. Oaksford and Chater, in particular, have developed many alternative normative accounts of reasoning over a period of years. They now take the position that everyday rationality is based on Bayesian decision theory, reflecting the uncertainty of the world we live in. People apply this everyday rationality in the laboratory and thus appear to make logical errors.

As an example, Oaksford and Chater have suggested that when people reason with conditional statements, they regard them as inherently uncertain. Consider the following problem as if it were presented prior to the US presidential election of 2016:

> If Donald Trump is elected president then the USA will build a wall across the Mexican border.
>
> Suppose that Donald Trump is elected president. Will the USA build a wall across the Mexican border?

In the traditional method, people would be asked for a yes or no answer. Related experiments suggest that many people would say no, even though the conclusion follows by the simple and valid *modus ponens* argument. Oaksford and Chater suggest, however, that it is rational for people to take account of their belief in the conditional. We can test this by allowing people to attach probabilities. Suppose someone believes that there is only a 30 per cent chance of Trump building his wall. This will make them reluctant to conclude for sure that he will do so. But if we allow them to give the conclusion a probability—now a common method—they will assign it 0.3. The mathematics is very simple in this instance, but Oaksford and Chater have shown support for this model across different kinds of conditional inferences, where the calculation of the correct probability is more complex.

The rational analysis approach of Oaksford and Chater is very much in the spirit of Cohen's famous critique. They endorse his view that apparent irrationality often reflects a wrong normative standard. They also implicitly agree with his arguments that psychological experiments may be artificial and subject to personal interpretation by the participants. For example, Oaksford and Chater famously argued that the choices given on the Wason selection task are rational. However, this depends upon people disregarding aspects of the standard instructions; they are assumed effectively to reinterpret the problem within the framework they use for everyday decision making. But there is a difficulty here that some critics have pointed out. It is always the case that *some* people give the traditionally correct answer on these laboratory problems, even ones as hard as the selection task. These people tend to have unusually high IQs, as I discuss a little later.

## Evolutionary approach

Evolutionary psychology made a big impact on the psychology of reasoning and decision making, when it was popularized by the writings of Leda Cosmides and John Tooby in the 1980s and 1990s. Their argument is that behaviour is rational because it has been shaped by evolution to be so. However, the environment in which we evolved is not that in which we now live. For most of our history, humans lived as hunter-gatherers in a hostile environment with scarce resources. Cosmides and Tooby controversially claimed that general reasoning ability could not have evolved, and that everything in human cognition is *modular*. A module is a self-contained section of the mind that developed for a specific purpose. The visual system is a good example. Our brains process information contained in the light received by our eyes, detecting lines, patterns, colours, and so on, and turning these, at a higher level, into representations of the world around us. All of this happens automatically with no intervention by the conscious person. In common with other modules, the processes of the visual system are dedicated to its function and inaccessible to any other part of the mind.

The idea of a modular mind was first introduced by the philosopher Jerry Fodor but he saw modules as coexisting with a general purpose reasoning system. It was the omission of such a general system that made Cosmides and Tooby's position so controversial, and Fodor was among their many critics. However, this 'massively modular' approach can explain why people solve problems in particular contexts and not in others, even if they have the same logical form. One example, mentioned in Chapter 5, is that of Bayesian reasoning and the ability to take account of base rate information. The evolutionary argument here is that we had no reason to evolve a module for thinking about probability but every reason to evolve a module for processing frequencies in the natural environment. The fact that people can solve frequency but not probability forms of Bayesian reasoning tasks was taken as evidence for their modular account of evolutionary rationality.

Cosmides' first work on reasoning focussed on the Wason selection task. We saw in Chapter 3 that in its standard abstract form the task is very difficult. However, there are realistic forms that are very easy, including the drinking age problem. Cosmides reviewed a number of published experiments and claimed that the easy forms all have something in common—they constitute *social contracts*. In a social contract, permission to perform an action depends on a precondition which is set by society. In the drinking age problem, anyone drinking alcohol must be of a minimum age, and if not they are cheating. Cosmides argued that in evolution it would have been very important to have enforceable social contracts and we would have evolved a module for detecting cheaters. Hence, people solving such versions are exhibiting evolutionary rationality. The failure of (most) people to solve the abstract selection task also supported her view that we did not evolve a general reasoning system. This theory shares the problem identified for the rational analysis approach, however. How is it that *some* people can solve the task, even if few in number?

One argument advanced by critics of the evolutionary theory was that there are solvable forms of the Wason task that are *not* social contracts. Manktelow and Over demonstrated one such, with the statement: 'If you clear up spilt blood then you must wear rubber gloves.' Almost everyone given this will check the people who are clearing up blood and the ones who are *not* wearing rubber gloves. But a person violating this rule is clearly not cheating anyone but themselves. Far from conceding defeat, however, the response of the evolutionary psychologists was to propose an alternative module for *hazard avoidance* which can explain success on this version and similar ones. Of course, one could argue that a theory which can construct ad hoc modules when required is not falsifiable. And exactly how strong is the argument that we *would have* evolved something, just because it is useful? Fodor, a leading critic of the massive modularity approach, has remarked ironically that he would have evolved a mechanism for navigating by the Earth's magnetic field, to help him find his way on cloudy nights!

## Fast and frugal heuristics

As discussed in Chapter 4, Kahneman and Tversky famously proposed a series of heuristics in probability judgement, such as availability and representativeness. Their papers on this tended to emphasize cases where such heuristics lead to error, so the research programme they inspired is often referred to as 'heuristics and biases'. In common with Wason, Kahneman and Tversky were subject to many attacks for apparently demonstrating or claiming that human beings are irrational. One of the earliest and leading critics was Gerd Gigerenzer, who believed that their experiments were unrepresentative and misleading. He was the first author to claim that many biases in statistical reasoning could be made to disappear by using frequencies instead of probabilities.

Gigerenzer leads a major school of research on human decision making and has a distinctive position on rationality. While closely related to the evolutionary approach, he is more focussed on *ecological* than evolutionary rationality. Ecological rationality means that we are adapted to the environment in which we operate. Of course, evolution may play a big part in this, but so too can learning and development. The ecological tradition has much older roots in psychology, and ecological psychologists believe that studying the environment as well as the individual is essential in order to understand human cognition. Gigerenzer also draws inspiration from Simon's work on bounded rationality. Whatever mechanisms we have developed for effective reasoning must be relatively simple and undemanding. We will not, for example, have internalized the mathematics of Bayes' theorem. While, like Oaksford and Chater, Gigerenzer takes rationality as a given, he does not seek alternative normative theories. In fact, he has argued that we are often better off relying on intuitions or 'gut feelings' rather than attempting to solve problems by conscious rule-based reasoning.

Gigerenzer and his school have conducted extensive work on what are known as 'fast and frugal' heuristics. The idea is that we have simple mechanisms that provide very effective decision making in our normal environments. Unlike Kahneman and Tversky's heuristics, these lead us to make good decisions rather than errors. A good example is the *recognition heuristic*. This is one among many items in the 'adaptive tool box', an idea closely related to Cosmides and Tooby's collection of cognitive modules.

The recognition heuristic is described as providing a benefit of ignorance. In fact, advocates of this approach have gone so far as to suggest that ignorance can outperform expertise when investing in stock markets. The essential definition of the recognition heuristic is that if one of two objects is recognized and the other not, then the recognized object has the higher value.

As an illustration, if both American and German students are asked to judge the relative size of American cities, and of German cities, the foreigners do better, despite having less knowledge. They just go for the one they have heard of. In one study, only 62 per cent of students at the University of Chicago correctly judged San Diego to be bigger than San Antonio, while 100 per cent of students at the University of Munich got it right. In another study, Turkish students predicted the outcome of English FA Cup games much better than English students who knew a lot more about the teams. Of course, the Turkish students chose big clubs like Manchester United, Liverpool, or Arsenal that they had heard of, and this turned out to be a better predictor than reasoning about the form of individual clubs and players. The value of the recognition heuristic in real environments has also been demonstrated by Gigerenzer's group in computer simulations.

While this work has produced some striking results, it leaves some important questions unanswered. For example, what mechanism in the mind is responsible for selecting the right heuristic from the toolbox for a particular job? And the idea that ignorance trumps knowledge is surely a dangerous one in many contexts. Do we really want our politicians to base their decisions on ignorance—regarding scientific research on climate change for example?

## Individual differences and intelligence

Some authors, like Cosmides and Gigerenzer, have sought to downplay the role of general intelligence and general purpose reasoning in achieving rationality. However, it is established by many years of work that there is a general factor in human intelligence—usually referred to by the single letter, $g$—that is highly heritable. This means that measures of $g$, such as the IQ test, are largely (but not entirely) determined by the gene pool of the individual's parents. $g$ is closely correlated with academic attainment and implicated in a wide range of cognitive tasks, especially those that require reasoning. So why would we have such a pervasive form of general intelligence if it were not of any value?

A leading author on reasoning and rationality is Keith Stanovich, whose position could not be more different from the authors I have discussed so far. Stanovich argues strongly for a general purpose reasoning system within a dual-process framework (Chapter 7). Together with his collaborator, Rich West, Stanovich has conducted a large number of studies of individual differences in performance on judgement, reasoning, and decision making tasks. Most of these studies rely on SAT scores as a measure of general intelligence. The SAT is a test taken by all students entering higher education in the USA. These scores are known to be highly correlated with IQ, even if self-reported, and are hence a good means for estimating $g$. The overwhelming finding of these studies is that general intelligence predicts correct performance on nearly all of these tasks, as assessed by the *standard* normative theories.

So while other authors seek to explain away errors and biases by use of alternative norms, or to downgrade the role of general purpose reasoning systems, Stanovich and West's work appears to point in the opposite direction. Whatever it is that intelligence tests measure makes people better at solving the kind of laboratory problems used to study thinking and decision making. But does this mean that people with high IQs are more rational? While Stanovich holds that standard norms provide a good working definition of rational behaviour, he does not actually equate rationality with general intelligence. In fact, he claims that to do so is to commit a dangerous fallacy. The reason is that IQ is not the *only* correlate of performance on these tasks. Individuals also differ in what are known as *rational thinking dispositions*. This means that some individuals are inclined to rely on intuitions while others make an effort to reason. Contrary to the claims of Gigerenzer, at least on these typical laboratory problems, reliance on intuition often leads to error. As a result, people of high IQ but low thinking disposition can sometimes fail to solve a simple problem. They rely on (a false) intuition rather than applying their power of reasoning.

In essence, Stanovich claims that rationality requires a combination of both general intelligence and a rational thinking disposition. He and West have been working towards development of a 'rationality quotient' (RQ) that will combine both elements. However, it is important to note that their methodology relies on standard normative performance, mostly on decision making tasks, as the criterion of rationality. As such the RQ might predict good performance for scientists, engineers, and economists, although even here it might not capture qualities of imagination and intuition that can be important for creativity. It seems less relevant to subjects such as music, literature, and arts generally where an intuitive style would be more productive. Even in fields such as management and politics, success does not just depend upon reasoning but requires good judgement. Whether the RQ would predict success in such fields is currently unknown.

## So are we rational?

Scientists working on the psychology of thinking have taken a number of different views on rationality. Clearly there is an issue to address, as participants in experiments on reasoning and decision making, usually of university-level intelligence, make many mistakes on these tasks. Not only that but they exhibit a number of cognitive biases. So it would be easy to claim on this basis that people are irrational. On the other hand, many philosophers and psychologists have taken the view that the human species is self-evidently highly intelligent and successful, so there must be something wrong with the experiments or their interpretation.

One clear area of dispute is the value of standard normative theory, such as logic and decision theory. Some authors rely on such theories for their standard working definition of rationality. Others say that if people make errors these theories must be wrong. Some want to replace standard theories with alternatives but others see little need for normative theory at all. Another issue is the value of the experimental tasks themselves—are they really a fair and appropriate way to measure 'everyday' rationality, outside of the laboratory? Perhaps the cognitive biases observed are just misapplications of normally adaptive mechanisms in an artificial context.

Another area of disagreement is the importance of general intelligence. Some authors in the evolutionary and ecological traditions seem to attach little importance to it and deny a useful role for a general purpose system of thinking and reasoning. But over a century of research on intelligence and IQ testing has established beyond doubt a robust, inherited general factor of intelligence that is correlated with performance on very many cognitive tasks. In the philosophical tradition, also, reasoning ability has been viewed as the cornerstone of rationality. More recent psychological research has established that both instrumental and epistemic rationality, defined by conventional means, are aided by a combination of general intelligence and rational thinking disposition.

Finally, it can be argued that psychologists have become too involved in arguments about rationality. The task of a cognitive psychologist, like any other scientist, is to understand the processes they study. A geologist studies how rocks are formed and transformed but makes no judgement as to whether they *ought* to behave in the way they do. Throughout most of cognitive psychology the same holds: we may observe visual illusions or biases in how the memory system works, but we do not judge people as irrational as a result. It is only in the sphere of 'higher' cognitive processes that we seem to feel the need to judge what we observe.

# Chapter 7
# From dual processes to two minds

As Sir Francis Galton understood, the great mass of brain work must be automatic because consciousness has such a limited capacity. It is a commonplace observation that we perform many of our tasks on 'automatic pilot'. Something as complex as driving a car through modern traffic can be performed with so little conscious attention that we may use the time to plan the day ahead, engage in conversation with a passenger, or listen to a radio play. This only applies to skills that are heavily practised, of course, and even then we *may* need at times to pay conscious attention. If a hazardous situation arises, for example when traffic ahead suddenly slows down, our attention will switch to the task of driving and we can no longer follow what is on the radio. This tells us some important things. First, while our conscious attention is elsewhere, some process in our brain is still monitoring the road situation for hazards and is able to call up conscious attention when required. Second, it shows us that our ability to think consciously is limited and we need to switch it away from one demanding task to perform another. If the competing task interferes with this, the distraction can be dangerous. For example, much evidence now suggests that use of mobile telephones while driving, even hands-free, can lead to accidents.

While consciousness dominated most philosophical work on thinking from the time of Aristotle, there were also some philosophers, from Plato onwards, who recognized forms of thinking without conscious awareness. Over the past fifty years or so, there has been a large amount of attention to dual processing in psychology but with many different theories and much variation in terminology. In this book, I have used the terms Type 1 to refer to thinking that is fast and intuitive, and Type 2 for thinking that is slow and reflective. Some modern psychologists, however, still refer to a distinction between conscious and nonconscious thinking, particularly in social psychology. One such is Tim Wilson, who has focussed much of his work on self-awareness. He describes much evidence that our conscious thinking has a limited role in controlling our behaviour, and that implicit attitudes and stereotypes have much bigger effects than we believe. In his 2002 book, *Strangers to Ourselves*, Wilson comments that the 'adaptive unconscious is more than a gatekeeper, deciding what information to admit to consciousness. It is also a spin doctor that interprets information outside of consciousness.'

There is a great deal of evidence in social psychology that even people who believe themselves to be unprejudiced and egalitarian nevertheless share cultural stereotypes with those who are overtly prejudiced. One study, conducted in the USA, borrowed a method from cognitive psychology called semantic priming. Suppose you are shown a string of letters on a computer screen and asked if it is a word. You can press a key for 'yes' and another for 'no', with your response time recorded. Imagine that two successive words are 'cat' and 'dog'. Response times for 'dog' will be faster than if the words were 'sky' and 'dog'. The target word 'dog' is said to be primed by another word of related meaning, like 'cat'.

In one social psychology study, the prime words were 'black' and 'white' but presented subliminally, so that they could not be consciously seen. Participants had no idea that their attitudes were being tested at all. The authors found that words that form part of the cultural stereotype for whites and blacks were primed by these subliminal cues but in different ways. When 'white' was used, people more quickly identified words that were positive associations in the white stereotype, such as intelligent and successful. There was, however, no priming effect for words that form a negative part of the stereotype for whites, such as greedy and materialistic. For the 'black' cue, however, the reverse was observed; only negative words in the stereotype (lazy, violent) and not the positive ones (athletic, religious) were primed. This implies a negative implicit attitude that most participants would not expect to hold. However, many similar findings have been reported.

If stereotypes operate at a Type 1 or nonconscious level, can they be suppressed by conscious Type 2 processing? Studies suggest that to an extent they can be, but only if the individual is aware that the implicit attitude is affecting their behaviour. Like other kinds of Type 2 processing discussed in this book, it requires conscious effort. Unfortunately, as we have also seen, Type 2 processing can sometimes be used to rationalize the results of unconscious biases. For example, a recruitment officer might give good reasons for preferring a candidate who is young, male, and white which are entirely related to the job in question and the candidate's merits. He might be quite unaware of any prejudice influencing his decision. Research actually shows that interviewers can be influenced by any number of features that would never be mentioned in an interviewer's report such as appearance, tone of voice, or even the strength of handshake.

Many cognitive psychologists avoid talking about consciousness at all, believing it to be a poorly defined concept. Thus many different terms have been used to describe Type 1 and Type 2 thinking. Some authors talk of intuitive and deliberative processing, others of automatic and controlled processing, and still others distinguish processing that is associative from that which is rule-based. Some contrast thinking which is heuristic (Type 1) with that which is systematic or analytic (Type 2). Whether all these theorists mean exactly the same thing by these distinctions is highly debatable. I will return to this problem later.

# Type 1 processing and the power of intuition

Dual-process theories in the psychology of thinking and reasoning have traditionally associated Type 1 thinking with various kinds of cognitive bias. It would be a mistake, however, to believe that Type 2 thinking is necessarily superior. It has special properties, to be sure, but it also has a very limited capacity and is relatively slow. The brain must carry out the vast majority of its processing automatically, rapidly, and outside of conscious awareness. Most of this processing is effective and helps us achieve our goals.

Consider again the example of driving a car while listening to a radio play. The latter is the main focus of our conscious attention until the driving becomes hazardous. So what is the brain also doing while we are enjoying the play? Here are just a few of the Type 1 processes in operation: visual processing of the road situation, motor control of the vehicle, and speech and language processing to understand what is being said on the radio. Each of these involves very complex and rapid processing that we could not do at the Type 2 level. Yes, we are conscious, if we attend to what the road looks like, what the characters in the play are saying, and what tone of voice they have. But we—conscious persons—have no idea how any of the prodigious feats of information processing that precede these conscious experiences are actually achieved.

When authors talk of intuition or intuitive thought, they are not generally referring to the kind of automated processing that underlies visual or speech processing. In the psychology of thinking and reasoning, Type 1 processing is more commonly used to refer to 'gut feelings' or inclinations which determine our decision making in the absence of conscious reflection. Some authors, like Gigerenzer, have suggested that we can often make better decisions by relying on such feelings than by the use of conscious reasoning. Note that this is exactly the *opposite* argument to the usual explanation of cognitive biases encountered in this book. Typically, Type 1 processes are described as faulty intuitions which have been used to explain cognitive biases, while slower and more effortful Type 2 reasoning is needed to get the right answer. How does this contradiction arise?

I think the key here is the role of *experiential learning*, also called implicit or associative learning. We learn continuously by experience without necessarily being conscious of doing so. Such learning can provide very effective intuitions to aid our decision making. In Chapter 2, I pointed out that expert problem solving and decision making often arises from fast pattern recognition processes rather than slow reflective reasoning. I described the case of the fire chief who called his men out of a burning building because his 'sixth sense' told him that something was wrong, even though he could not consciously identify what it was. Experts, like everyone else, have two different kinds of knowledge. When doctors train in medical school, for example, they acquire a great deal of explicit knowledge about medical conditions and their treatments through book learning. They will need to call on this early in their careers and also later when presented with unusual cases. However, when a doctor practises medicine, they also acquire a great deal of implicit knowledge by experiential learning. An experienced general practitioner will not need to recall textbook learning when confronted with a common set of symptoms. She will just know from experience what the cause is likely to be and how to treat it. In the same way, an experienced police detective will usually know when a suspect is lying, but they did not learn this from a lecture or a textbook.

Implicit learning of associations and patterns happens to all of us, all the time, without any conscious effort to learn. In fact, Arthur Reber, who has conducted many studies of implicit learning, has shown that *trying* to learn complex patterns can sometimes be counterproductive. This is the kind of distinction that authors have in mind when they talk about (implicit) associative and (explicit) rule-based processing. Implicit or associative processing prevails when patterns are complex and difficult to describe as simple rules that can be applied consciously. Malcolm Gladwell, in his popular book *Blink*, cites examples such as an art expert who knew that a statue was fake but could not articulate how he knew and what was wrong with it. He also talks of a marriage guidance counsellor who could predict with high accuracy the success of a marriage after just one fifteen-minute counselling session. These experts are responding to patterns, which may be quite complex sets of cues whose meaning has been acquired by experience. The learning was implicit, the knowledge is implicit, and so the expert experiences what we call an intuition. That is a *feeling*, without a conscious rationale to support it. This is something quite different from learning explicit rules and applying them consciously by Type 2 reasoning.

So why are intuition and Type 1 processing so often blamed for cognitive biases in the laboratory? The reason is that the problems that psychologists present tend to be novel and also quite abstract in nature. Normally participants have no helpful prior experience to bring to these tasks, or if they do they are intentionally excluded. For example, people with training in logic are not allowed to take part in deductive reasoning experiments, or have their data discounted. Sometimes the problems are also designed so that prior knowledge will actually make it *harder* to solve them. In the belief bias paradigm, for example, people are presented with syllogisms which require quite difficult reasoning to solve. The task is set up so that some conclusions will be believable and others unbelievable, but this will be independent of the logical validity they are told to judge. So in this case, if the person goes on whether the conclusion feels right or wrong, they will show a belief bias.

## Type 2 thinking, intelligence, and working memory

Type 2 thinking—conscious reflection—comes into its own when problems combine complexity with novelty and cannot be solved by applying relevant experience. Such problems require explicit, conscious, effortful *reasoning* to solve. Because of the interest in this type of reasoning, many laboratory tasks are deliberately designed to require it. In the laboratory, participants often struggle with such tasks, making so many mistakes as to have led to the rationality debate discussed in Chapter 6. One thing that studying such tasks has clearly shown is that people of high IQ are more able to solve most of them. We have also learned more about what kind of problems need Type 2 reasoning to solve. They usually require what I call hypothetical thinking and what Stanovich calls 'cognitive decoupling'. This means that people have to conduct mental simulations and to detach or disregard what they already know and believe.

While most decisions are made on the basis of habit and experience, Type 2 thinking is required when we need to imagine and compare future consequences of our actions. How do we decide how to control global warming or what the economic consequences are of a country joining or extracting itself from a trade deal? Such decisions tax our powers of Type 2 thinking to the limit. This thinking appears to be slow, effortful, detached, and can essentially deal with only one thing at a time. If it is really distinctive from the bulk of our cognitive processing, then there must be some special mechanism in the human mind which allows it to happen. A clue as to what this is has arisen from the study of memory. In fact, over the past forty to fifty years, when dual-process theories were being developed in cognitive and social psychology, an entirely parallel field of work was being carried out by memory researchers. It was only relatively recently that the connection between the two became apparent.

In the 1960s, memory researchers made a clear distinction between short-term and long-term memory, terms which are used differently in popular culture. To a psychologist, short-term memory persists only for a few seconds, unless consciously rehearsed, and has a sharply limited storage capacity. In the early 1970s, Alan Baddeley and his colleagues realized that this short-term store played an extremely important role in human cognition, allowing information to be kept temporarily for further processing, such as transfer to long-term memory, language processing, or reasoning. They coined the term *working memory* to reflect these properties, and launched a major field of study which has flourished ever since.

The parallel studies of reasoning and working memory began to include measures of individual differences in the past twenty years or so. What many of us had suspected in the study of reasoning and decision making was confirmed: measures of general intelligence predicted success on most of these laboratory tasks. Meanwhile, memory researchers started to measure *working memory capacity* by seeing how many items people could hold in short-term memory while performing another, unrelated cognitive task. It was quickly discovered that working memory capacity varies considerably across individuals and predicts performance on a very wide range of cognitive tasks. Soon it was also discovered that this measure correlates very highly with general intelligence measures such as IQ, as well as with reasoning ability.

The connection between Type 2 thinking and working memory is not just based on individual differences. Type 2 thought has been described by thinking and reasoning researchers as slow, conscious, sequential, and limited in capacity—all properties separately identified for working memory. In recent years, psychologists working on reasoning and decision making have shown that people of higher working memory capacity reason differently from those of lower capacity—their reasoning is more abstract and less belief-based, for example. Reasoning researchers have also given people working memory loads—items to remember while reasoning—and showed that this causes cognitive biases to increase and correct solutions to decrease on various tasks. The inference here is that such loads interfere with Type 2 but not Type 1 reasoning, because only the former relies on working memory.

Type 1 reasoning is very hard to define as there seem to be many systems in the brain which operate autonomously and in parallel. A definition of Type 2 processing now seems much clearer, however. In a recent paper, Stanovich and I replied to a number of criticisms of dual-process theory that have been published in recent years. One of these is that the theory tends to be vague and ill-defined. We defined Type 2 processing as that which (a) engages working memory and (b) involves hypothetical thinking or cognitive decoupling. That is, the ability to reason about possibilities, while ignoring what you know to be actually true.

## How can dual-process theories explain cognitive biases?

Most dual-process theorists assume that (a) Type 1 processes operate quickly, leading to intuitive responses to problems, but that (b) these potential answers may be altered as a result of subsequent Type 2 reasoning. Sometimes checking of the initial intuition leads only to justification or rationalization, as was observed in early studies of the Wason selection task (Chapter 3). This task has an exceptionally high error rate, however. On problems where people are more successful, the theorists claim that people may find fault with their initial intuitions and engage in more careful reasoning. As a result they may avoid a bias and give a correct answer. A lot of research has focussed on when such intervention by reasoning will occur and when it will be successful. This general approach has been taken by Stanovich, Kahneman, and myself, among others.

Stanovich has pointed out that if people are to solve one of these problems they must first perceive a need to reason. He suggests that we are by nature 'cognitive misers' who only expend effort on reasoning when we are well motivated to do so. Intuitive answers can be so compelling that we seem never to engage in reasoning at all. This was demonstrated by Frederick in a simple three-item test known as the cognitive reflection test, or CRT.

We met one of these items—the bat and ball problem—in Chapter 2. Here is another:

If it takes 5 machines 5 minutes to make 5 widgets, how long would it take 100 machines to make 100 widgets?

The intuitive answer, 100 minutes, comes straight to mind and many people, even of high IQ, give this without apparently thinking about the problem at all. A little thought will reveal that each machine takes 5 minutes to make a widget, so that is how long 100 machines will take to make 100 widgets.

Tasks like this have been studied by Valerie Thompson and colleagues, who have shown that people are less likely to engage in reasoning if they have a strong feeling of confidence in the intuitive answer. She invented an ingenious method to study this, called the two response task. Participants are given a reasoning or decision problem and asked to make a fast, intuitive response. They then rate how confident they are that the answer was correct, which she calls *feeling of rightness* (FOR). Then they are asked to think again about the problem for as long as they like and give a second answer which can be different.

Her main finding is that when initial confidence or FOR is high, people spend less time rethinking the problem and are less likely to change the answer. Whether or not people check their intuitions with reasoning also depends on their 'cognitive style'—a trait measured by a number of scales referred to collectively as *rational thinking dispositions*. Some people are generally disposed to rely on their intuitions and others are more inclined to check them by reasoning. Stanovich and West have made extensive use of these scales in their studies, as well as a measure of general intelligence. They find generally that people are more successful on such tasks (a) when they have higher intelligence and also (b) when they have a higher disposition for rational reasoning. As Stanovich points out, we may also need relevant training and knowledge for some kinds of reasoning—which he calls *mindware*. For example, people with training in mathematics and statistics will perform better when reasoning about numbers and probabilities and show fewer cognitive biases.

Not all dual-process theories have a sequential form, in which intuitions precede reasoning. Some authors have suggested instead that there are parallel forms of thinking that may produce different answers and compete with each other. These two kinds of processing are typically described as rule-based (Type 2) and associative (Type 1). Suppose you are choosing somewhere to eat in a strange town. You see a familiar franchise in which you have often eaten before in different cities with satisfactory results. Associative processing would give you a positive feeling and inclination to choose that restaurant. But also suppose that you had done a web search before leaving your hotel and seen negative recent reviews of that particular restaurant. Rule-based reasoning might then lead to an opposite conclusion: 'Web reviews are usually reliable, these reviews are negative, so I probably will not enjoy the meal.' In this case, the two forms of processing would be in conflict, pulling you in different directions.

This kind of theory can be applied to standard laboratory tasks as well. Hence in syllogistic reasoning there might be a conflict between rule-based reasoning and associative belief bias. The technical question is whether the processes operate in parallel, or in sequence. There are ways of trying to resolve this issue but describing them is beyond the scope of this book.

## Is there one general theory of dual processing?

Over the past twenty years or so, a number of authors, including Stanovich and myself, have listed common features of dual-process theories such as those shown in Table 3. There clearly are close family resemblances between such theories, and a number of authors describe some, but not necessarily all, of the features

**Table 3** Features often associated with two types of processing in dual-process theories, with additional features often associated with two systems or two minds

| Type 1 process (intuitive) | Type 2 process (reflective) |
|---|---|
| Fast | Slow |
| High capacity | Capacity limited |
| Parallel | Serial |
| Belief-based | Abstract |
| Nonconscious | Conscious |
| Biased responses | Normative responses |
| Contextualized | Abstract |
| Automatic | Controlled |
| Associative | Rule-based |
| Implicit learning and knowledge | Explicit learning and knowledge |
| Experience-based decision making | Consequential decision making |
| Independent of cognitive ability | Correlated with cognitive ability |
| *Independent of working memory* | *Requires working memory* |
| *Autonomous* | *Cognitive decoupling and mental simulation* |
| **System 1 (old mind)** | **System 2 (new mind)** |
| Evolved early | Evolved late |
| Similar to animal cognition | Distinctively human |
| Implicit knowledge | Explicit knowledge |
| Basic emotions | Complex emotions |

Italicized attributes described as defining features by Evans and Stanovich.

I show here. This has led to what we call a 'received' theory of dual processing which incorporates all of these features as if there were just one theory out there that all authors agreed about. Several recent high-profile papers have been published criticizing dual-process theory which appear to be directed more against this received theory rather than individual accounts. In particular, critics point (correctly) to evidence that sometimes the features on that list are not observed together. As an example, consider the relation of Type 1 and 2 processing to bias and correct solutions.

I have already made it clear that while Type 1 processing *typically* leads to biases and Type 2 processing *typically* leads to correct answers in laboratory tasks, there is no necessary reason why that should happen. Type 1 intuitions can be helpful where people have relevant experience, or when other intuitive cues lead to the correct answer, and Type 2 reasoning can fail because people have insufficient capacity to reason or lack the relevant knowledge. Nevertheless, some authors talk as though we could diagnose the type of processing from the correctness of the answer. For example, researchers have reported that correct (as well as biased) answers can be intuitively compelling and have presented this as a problem for dual-process theory. In one recent study, by Simon Handley and others, people were given simple reasoning problems involving *modus ponens* arguments, in which belief and logic could be put in conflict. For example:

> If a child is crying then he is happy.
> Suppose a child is crying. Is he happy?

If we substitute 'sad' for 'happy' there is no longer a conflict. Many previous studies showed that when people are instructed to make logical inferences such conflicts interfere. The novelty here was that people were also instructed, in a separate task, to decide whether or not the conclusion was *believable*. Curiously, the logic of the inference interfered with belief judgements as well. For example, when there is a valid inference that the child is happy, it takes longer to conclude that he is not, on the basis of belief. Hence it seems that 'logical intuitions' interfere with belief judgement in just the same way as belief interferes with validity judgements. This finding is very interesting, but we must not assume that valid inferences necessarily require Type 2 processing or that Type 1 processes are only belief-based. *Modus ponens* is very simple and may follow immediately from understanding the word 'if'. Drawing this inference does not tax working memory, so why should this also not be intuitive? It could be that really two intuitions or Type 1 processes are in conflict here.

Stanovich and I concede that there are problems with dual-process theories, but we would assert that the received dual-process theory is a straw man which no one author has actually proposed. This general theory appears to be present in the minds of some supporters as well as critics of the approach, but is not a real entity to be attacked. The typical features are just that. The only necessary and defining ones, we suggest, are the links to working memory and hypothetical thinking already discussed.

## Two minds theory

A number of authors, including Seymour Epstein, Arthur Reber, Keith Stanovich, David Over, and myself have suggested at various times that there might be an implicit system (or System 1) which is evolutionarily ancient and shared with other animals, and an explicit system (or System 2) which is predominantly or distinctively human. It has become clear now, however, that System 2 is not *exclusively* human. Animals also have a form of working memory and controlled attention, for example. But clearly powers of hypothetical thinking are far better developed in humans than other animals. Our intellectual achievements tower above all other species.

The idea that Type 1 processing is animal-like comes particularly from studies of experiential learning. By focussing on conditioning and associative learning, the behaviourists missed key features of human cognition. But these older forms of learning are part of the human mind too. In my own version of two minds theory, this kind of learning forms part of the old (intuitive) mind, while the new (reflective) mind is associated with reasoning and hypothetical thinking. This theory is supported by the writings of the cognitive archaeologist, Steve Mithen. He claims that the general learning system in ancient humans was supplemented by the development of specialized intelligences in early humans to deal with social exchanges, the natural environment, tool making, and language. Uniquely among hominid species, however, modern humans then evolved a kind of flexible intelligence that allowed us to make connections across different domains and engage in general reasoning. This flexible intelligence corresponds broadly with the new mind.

Now I much prefer to talk of the old and new minds than of System 1 and System 2, as each mind evidently has multiple systems and the new mind relies on Type 1 as well as Type 2 processing. Among the specialized intelligences, or cognitive modules, that we possess, some are largely shared with other animals. These include associative learning and much of our visual system. But several modules are uniquely human and the new mind could not function without them. I have already mentioned one—language. Another is called meta-representation or 'theory of mind'. We can imagine and consider other people's thoughts and feelings, and 'read' their minds from their behaviour and the context. This makes us socially very advanced and only the most rudimentary aspects of such a facility have been found in some of the apes. But like other cognitive modules these function mostly autonomously. We can easily understand layers of these representations, as when someone says to us: 'Paul is upset because he believes that Mary no longer loves him.' We might reply: 'That is typical of Paul, he is so insecure', adding our belief about Paul's belief about Mary's state of mind. One form of evidence that this extraordinary facility uses a specialized built-in module is that it appears to be absent or highly deficient in autistic people.

According to two minds theory, the new mind was added to the old, which is still present, so that the two have different mechanisms which may come into conflict. Most of the time the two minds work well together as we go about our lives relying on numerous autonomous systems of ancient as well as more recent origin. But when things go badly wrong, we become aware of the conflict. We may have a compulsive behavioural addiction, like gambling, that we cannot break even though we know it is ruining our lives. We may develop phobias which prevent us from travelling to see a sick parent, or using a lift to reach an important meeting in a tall building. Thus the old mind can sometimes frustrate the goals of the new mind.

In my theory, the two minds also have a different kind of rationality. The old mind achieves its goals by responding to the past. Old mind learning and conditioning involve repeating what has worked before, as is typical of animal cognition. But the new mind looks to the future and tries to make decisions by mental simulations—imagining and reasoning about the future consequences of our actions. As dual-process research shows, such reasoning is difficult and effortful and our behaviour often reflects our habits and intuitions instead. As an example, only consequential reasoning and decision making will enable us to save the world from global warming. We cannot learn from the experience of a disaster that lies in the future. Whether we will actually be able to change our established behaviour sufficiently based on this reasoning is far from clear.

## Final thoughts

Dual-process theories of various kinds have been widespread in the academic literature on thinking, reasoning, and decision making (as well as in social psychology) for many years. While there are family resemblances between theories (Table 3), the temptation to assume a single 'received' theory underlying all of these should be avoided. In the study of thinking and reasoning, dual-process accounts have mostly been applied to the explanation of cognitive biases. However, Type 1 processing can give the right answer and Type 2 can be wrong. It is simply that the typical laboratory tasks are designed to require Type 2 processing for their solution and generally to preclude relevant prior experience that could provide helpful Type 1 intuitions.

I leave the reader with a final thought. The working memory/Type 2 system is what enabled modern humans to develop the kind of flexible intelligence of which Mithen talks, and which I call the new mind. We have to hold different information in mind simultaneously, to think about what kind of hunting tool would deal with a new predator for example. We have a much more powerful version of this working memory system than other animals because of the huge enlargement of the frontal lobes that occurred at some point in the evolution of modern humans, for reasons unknown. Also, for reasons on which we can only speculate, we modern humans evolved a very powerful form of representational language and the capacity to think about thoughts. The combination of all of these things allowed our species to develop its remarkable form of intelligence that sets us apart from all other animals.

# Appendix

## Bayes' theorem

Bayes' theorem is a simple proof in probability theory that has wide ramifications. The following equation in the probability calculus shows that the probability of the conjunction of two events A and B is equal to the probability of A times the conditional probability of B given A:

$$P(A \ \& \ B) = P(A).P(B \ / \ A)$$

From this we can derive the following equation, a form of Bayes' theorem when we have two alternative hypotheses H1 and H2, and piece of evidence, or datum D:

$$\frac{P(H1 \ / \ D)}{P(H2 \ / \ D)} = \frac{P(H1)}{P(H2)} \times \frac{P(D \ / \ H1)}{P(D \ / \ H2)}$$

These three terms can be given the following verbal interpretation

Posterior odds = Prior odds × Likelihood ratio

This equation is the foundation of Bayesian philosophy in which probabilities are subjective and represent beliefs. The prior odds are the beliefs we hold before we examine evidence and the equation shows us how to revise those beliefs after we encounter the evidence.

Consider the case of the medical diagnosis problem described in Chapter 5. H1 = patient has the disease and H2 = patient does not have the disease. The posterior odds in this case express the chances of having the disease *after* the evidence (diagnostic test D) has been presented. The prior odds (reflecting the base rate specified) of having the disease are 1:999. The likelihood ratio, which expresses the diagnosticity of the evidence, is the true positive rate divided by the false positive rate, in this case 100:5. The product of these two ratios gives us approximately 1:50 as the posterior odds. Hence, the chance of having the disease is about 2 per cent, as demonstrated intuitively in the text.

# References

## Chapter 1: Introduction and history

Chomsky, N. (1959). A review of B. F. Skinner's *Verbal behavior*. *Language, 35,* 25–58.

Galton, F. (1893). *Inquiries into human faculty and its development*. London: Macmillan.

Hall, C. (1954/1999). *A primer of Freudian psychology*. New York: Penguin.

James, W. (1890/2007). *The principles of psychology*. New York: Cosimo.

Mandler, G. (2006). *A history of modern experimental psychology: From James and Wundt to cognitive science*. Cambridge, MA: MIT Press.

Nisbett, R. E., and Wilson, T. D. (1977). Telling more than we can know: Verbal reports on mental processes. *Psychological Review, 84,* 231–95.

Singh, S. (2010). *The code book: The secret history of codes and code breaking*. London: Fourth Estate.

Skinner, B. F. (1957). *Verbal behavior*. Englewood Cliffs, NJ: Prentice-Hall.

Watson, J. B. (1913). Psychology as the behaviorist sees it. *Psychological Review, 20,* 158–77.

Winters, B., et al. (2012). Diagnostic errors in the intensive care unit: a systematic review of autopsy studies. *British Medical Journal Quality & Safety, 21,* 894–902.

## Chapter 2: Problem solving

Duncker, K. (1945). On problem solving. *Psychological Monographs*, *58*, No. 270, 1–113.

Evans, J. St B. T., and Stanovich, K. E. (2013). Dual process theories of higher cognition: Advancing the debate. *Perspectives on Psychological Science*, *8*, 223–41.

Frederick, S. (2005). Cognitive reflection and decision making. *Journal of Economic Perspectives*, *19*, 25–42.

Gick, M. L., and Holyoak, K. J. (1980). Analogical problem solving. *Cognitive Psychology*, *12*, 306–55.

Gilhooly, K. J., Ball, L. J., and Macchi, L. (Eds) (2015). *Creativity and insight in problem solving*. Special issue of *Thinking & Reasoning*, *21* (1). Abingdon: Taylor and Francis.

Kasparov, G. (2011). *Kasparov on Kasparov, Part 1*. Guildford, CT: Everyman.

Klein, G. (1998). *Sources of power*. Cambridge, MA: MIT Press.

Mithen, S. (1996). *The prehistory of the mind*. London: Thames & Hudson.

Newell, A., and Simon, H. A. (1972). *Human problem solving*. Englewood Cliffs, NJ: Prentice-Hall.

Robertson, S. I. (2001). *Problem solving*. Hove: Psychology Press.

Wertheimer, M. (1961). *Productive thinking*. London: Tavistock.

## Chapter 3: Thinking hypothetically

Byrne, R. M. J. (2005). *The rational imagination*. Cambridge, MA: MIT Press.

Evans, J. St B. T. (2016). A brief history of the Wason selection task. In N. Galbraith (Ed.), *The thinking mind: A festschrift for Ken Manktelow* (pp. 1–14). Hove: Psychology Press.

Evans, J. St B. T. (2016). Reasoning, biases and dual processes: The lasting impact of Wason (1960). *Quarterly Journal of Experimental Psychology*, *69*, 2076–92.

Evans, J. St B. T., and Over, D. E. (2004). *If*. Oxford: Oxford University Press.

Fugelsang, J. A., Stein, C. B., Green, A. E., and Dunbar, K. N. (2004). Theory and data interactions of the scientific mind: Evidence from the molecular and cognitive laboratory. *Canadian Journal of Experimental Psychology*, *58*, 86–95.

Lucas, E. J., and Ball, L. J. (2005). Think-aloud protocols and the selection task: Evidence for relevance effects and rationalisation processes. *Thinking and Reasoning, 11,* 35–66.

Sloman, S. A. (2005). *Causal models.* Oxford: Oxford University Press.

Wagenaar, W. A. (1988). *Paradoxes of gambling behaviour.* Hove and London: Erlbaum.

Wason, P. C., and Evans, J. St B. T. (1975). Dual processes in reasoning? *Cognition, 3,* 141–54.

White, P. A. (2003). Causal judgement as evaluation of evidence: The use of confirmatory and disconfirmatory information. *Quarterly Journal of Experimental Psychology, 56A,* 491–513.

## Chapter 4: Decision making

Baron, J., and Ritov, I. (2004). Omission bias, individual differences, and normality. *Organizational Behavior and Human Decision Processes, 94,* 74–85.

Bueler, R., Griffin, D., and Ross, M. (2002). Inside the planning fallacy: The causes and consequences of optimistic time predictions. In T. Gilovich, D. Griffin, and D. Kahneman (Eds), *Heuristics and biases: The psychology of intuitive judgement* (pp. 250–70). Cambridge: Cambridge University Press.

Evans, J. St B. T. (2007). *Hypothetical thinking: Dual processes in reasoning and judgement.* Hove: Psychology Press.

Gigerenzer, G. (2007). *Gut feelings: The intelligence of the unconscious.* London: Penguin.

Gigerenzer, G., and Todd, P. M. (1999). Fast and frugal heuristics: The adaptive toolbox. In G. Gigerenzer, P. M. Todd, and ABC Research Group (Eds), *Simple heuristics that make us smart* (pp. 3–36). New York: Oxford University Press.

Gilovich, T., Griffin, D., and Kahneman, D. (2002). *Heuristics and biases: The psychology of intuitive judgement.* Cambridge: Cambridge University Press.

Griffin, D., and Tversky, A. (1992). The weighting of evidence and the determinants of confidence. *Cognitive Psychology, 24,* 411–35.

Kahneman, D., Slovic, P., and Tversky, A. (1982). *Judgment under uncertainty: Heuristics and biases.* Cambridge: Cambridge University Press.

Kahneman, D., and Tversky, A. (1979). Prospect theory: An analysis of decision under risk. *Econometrica, 47,* 263–91.

Raylu, N., and Oci, T. P. S. (2002). Pathological gambling: A comprehensive review. *Clinical Psychology Review, 22*, 1009–61.

Shafir, E., Simenson, I., and Tversky, A. (1993). Reason-based choice. *Cognition, 49*, 11–36.

Soman, D. (2005). Framing, loss aversion and mental accounting. In D. J. Koehler and N. Harvey (Eds), *Blackwell handbook of judgment and decision making* (pp. 379–98). Oxford: Blackwell.

Tversky, A., and Kahneman, A. (1992). Advances in prospect theory: Cumulative representation of uncertainty. *Journal of Risk and Uncertainty, 5*, 297–323.

## Chapter 5: Reasoning

Barbey, A. K., and Sloman, S. A. (2007). Base-rate respect: From ecological validity to dual processes. *Behavioral and Brain Sciences, 30*, 241–97.

Braine, M. D. S., and O'Brien, D. P. (Eds) (1998). *Mental logic*. Mahwah, NJ: Lawrence Erlbaum Associates.

Byrne, R. M. J. (1991). Can valid inferences be suppressed? *Cognition, 39*, 71–8.

Cascells, W., Schoenburger, A., and Graboys, T. B. (1978). Interpretation by physicians of clinical laboratory results. *New England Journal of Medicine, 299*, 999–1001.

Cosmides, L., and Tooby, J. (1996). Are humans good intuitive statisticians after all? Rethinking some conclusions from the literature on judgment under uncertainty. *Cognition, 58*, 1–73.

Edgington, D. (2003). What if? Questions about conditionals. *Mind & Language, 18*, 380–401.

Evans, J. St B. T. (2002). Logic and human reasoning: An assessment of the deduction paradigm. *Psychological Bulletin, 128*, 978–96.

Evans, J. St B. T., Barston, J. L., and Pollard, P. (1983). On the conflict between logic and belief in syllogistic reasoning. *Memory & Cognition, 11*, 295–306.

Evans, J. St B. T., Handley, S. J., Harper, C., and Johnson-Laird, P. N. (1999). Reasoning about necessity and possibility: A test of the mental model debate. *Journal of Experimental Psychology: Learning, Memory and Cognition, 25*, 1495–513.

Gigerenzer, G. (2002). *Reckoning with risk*. London: Penguin Books.

Howson, C., and Urbach, P. (2006). *Scientific reasoning: The Bayesian approach* (3rd edition). Chicago: Open Court.

Johnson-Laird, P. N. (1983). *Mental models*. Cambridge: Cambridge University Press.

Johnson-Laird, P. N., and Savary, F. (1999). Illusory inferences: A novel class of erroneous deductions. *Cognition, 71*, 191–299.

Klauer, K. C., Musch, J., and Naumer, B. (2000). On belief bias in syllogistic reasoning. *Psychological Review, 107*, 852–84.

Oaksford, M., and Chater, N. (2007). *Bayesian rationality: The probabilistic approach to human reasoning*. Oxford: Oxford University Press.

Over, D. E., Hadjichristidis, C., Evans, J. St B. T., Handley, S. J., and Sloman, S. A. (2007). The probability of causal conditionals. *Cognitive Psychology, 54*, 62–97.

## Chapter 6: Are we rational?

Anderson, J. R. (1990). *The adaptive character of thought*. Hillsdale, NJ: Erlbaum.

Barkow, J. H., Cosmides, L., and Tooby, J. (Eds) (1992). *The adapted mind: Evolutionary psychology and the generation of culture*. Oxford: Oxford University Press.

Cohen, L. J. (1981). Can human irrationality be experimentally demonstrated? *Behavioral and Brain Sciences, 4*, 317–70.

Cosmides, L. (1989). The logic of social exchange: Has natural selection shaped how humans reason? *Cognition, 31*, 187–276.

Cosmides, L., and Tooby, J. (1996). Are humans good intuitive statisticians after all? Rethinking some conclusions from the literature on judgment under uncertainty. *Cognition, 58*, 1–73.

Elqayam, S., and Evans, J. St B. T. (2011). Subtracting 'ought' from 'is': Descriptivism versus normativism in the study of human thinking. *Behavioral and Brain Sciences, 34*, 233–90.

Evans, J. St B. T. (2007). *Hypothetical thinking: Dual processes in reasoning and judgement*. Hove: Psychology Press.

Evans, J. St B. T., and Over, D. E. (1996). *Rationality and reasoning*. Hove: Psychology Press.

Fiddick, L., Cosmides, L., and Tooby, J. (2000). No interpretation without representation: The role of domain-specific representations and inferences in the Wason selection task. *Cognition, 77*, 1–79.

Fodor, J. (1983). *The modularity of mind*. Scranton, PA: Crowell.

Fodor, J. (2001). *The mind doesn't work that way*. Cambridge, MA: MIT Press.

Gigerenzer, G. (2002). *Reckoning with risk*. London: Penguin Books.

Gigerenzer, G. (2007). *Gut feelings: The intelligence of the unconscious*. London: Penguin.

Gigerenzer, G., Todd, P. M., and ABC Research Group (1999). *Simple heuristics that make us smart*. New York and Oxford: Oxford University Press.

Manktelow, K. I., and Over, D. E. (1991). Social roles and utilities in reasoning with deontic conditionals. *Cognition*, *39*, 85–105.

Oaksford, M., and Chater, N. (1994). A rational analysis of the selection task as optimal data selection. *Psychological Review*, *101*, 608–31.

Oaksford, M., and Chater, N. (2007). *Bayesian rationality: The probabilistic approach to human reasoning*. Oxford: Oxford University Press.

Poletiek, F. (2001). *Hypothesis-testing behaviour*. Hove: Psychology Press.

Stanovich, K. E. (2011). *Rationality and the reflective mind*. New York: Oxford University Press.

Stanovich, K. E., West, R. W., and Toplack, M. E. (2016). *The rationality quotient: Towards a test of rational thinking*. Cambridge, MA: MIT Press.

## Chapter 7: From dual processes to two minds

Baddeley, A. (2007). *Working memory, thought and action*. Oxford: Oxford University Press.

Colom, R., Rebollo, I., Palacios, A., Juan-Espinosa, M., and Kyllonen, P. C. (2004). Working memory is (almost) perfectly predicted by g. *Intelligence*, *32* (3), 277–96.

De Neys, W. (2012). Bias and conflict: A case for logical intuitions. *Perspectives on Psychological Science*, *7*, 28–38.

Evans, J. St B. T. (2007). *Hypothetical thinking: Dual processes in reasoning and judgement*. Hove: Psychology Press.

Evans, J. St B. T. (2010). *Thinking twice: Two minds in one brain*. Oxford: Oxford University Press.

Evans, J. St B. T., and Stanovich, K. E. (2013). Dual process theories of higher cognition: Advancing the debate. *Perspectives on Psychological Science*, *8*, 223–41.

Frederick, S. (2005). Cognitive reflection and decision making. *Journal of Economic Perspectives*, *19*, 25–42.

Gladwell, M. (2005). *Blink*. London: Penguin.

Handley, S. J., Newstead, S. E., and Trippas, D. (2011). Logic, beliefs, and instruction: A test of the default interventionist account of belief bias. *Journal of Experimental Psychology-Learning Memory and Cognition, 37*, 28–43.

Keren, G., and Schul, Y. (2009). Two is not always better than one: A critical evaluation of two-system theories. *Perspectives on Psychological Science, 4*, 533–50.

Klein, G. (1998). *Sources of power*. Cambridge, MA: MIT Press.

Kruglanski, A. W., and Gigerenzer, G. (2011). Intuitive and deliberative judgements are based on common principles. *Psychological Review, 118*, 97–109.

Mithen, S. (1996). *The prehistory of the mind*. London: Thames & Hudson.

Reber, A. S. (1993). *Implicit learning and tacit knowledge*. Oxford: Oxford University Press.

Sloman, S. A. (1996). The empirical case for two systems of reasoning. *Psychological Bulletin, 119*, 3–22.

Smith, E., and DeCoster, J. (2000). Dual-process models in social and cognitive psychology: Conceptual integration and links to underlying memory systems. *Personality and Social Psychology Review, 4*, 108–31.

Stanovich, K. E. (2011). *Rationality and the reflective mind*. New York: Oxford University Press.

Toates, F. (2006). A model of the hierarchy of behaviour, cognition and consciousness. *Consciousness and Cognition, 15*, 75–118.

Thompson, V. A., Prowse Turner, J. A., and Pennycook, G. (2011). Intuition, reason, and metacognition. *Cognitive Psychology, 63*, 107–40.

Wilson, T. D. (2002). *Strangers to ourselves*. Cambridge, MA: Belknap Press.

# Further reading

For those wishing to explore topics in greater depth, I include some suggestions for further reading on each chapter. I have tried to choose publications that are relatively recent and accessible and also not too technically written. Mostly these are different from the sources listed in the References, although in a small number of cases a reference was also suitable for further reading. A couple of readings are broad enough to merit entry under more than one chapter heading.

## Chapter 1: Introduction and history

Mandler, G. (2006). *A history of modern experimental psychology: From James and Wundt to cognitive science.* Cambridge, MA: MIT Press.

Skinner, B. F. (1988). *About behaviorism.* New York: Random House.

Wertheimer, M. (2012). *A brief history of psychology* (5th edition). New York: Psychology Press.

## Chapter 2: Problem solving

Bassock, M., and Novick, L. R. (2012). Probem solving. In K. Holyoak and R. G. Morrison (Eds), *The Oxford handbook of thinking and reasoning* (pp. 412–32). Oxford: Oxford University Press.

Eysenck, M. W. and Keane, M. (2015). *Cognitive Psychology* (7th edition). Hove: Psychology Press, chapter 12, 'Problem solving and expertise'.

Van Steenburg, J., Fleck, I., Beeman, M., and Kounis, J. (2012). Insight. In K. Holyoak and R. G. Morrison (Eds), *The Oxford handbook of thinking and reasoning* (pp. 475–91). Oxford: Oxford University Press.

## Chapter 3: Thinking hypothetically

Byrne, R. M. J. (2016). Counterfactual thought. *Annual Review of Psychology, 67*, 135–57.

Evans, J. St B. T. (2007*). Hypothetical thinking: Dual processes in reasoning and judgement.* Hove. Psychology Press.

Evans, J. St B. T. (2016). A brief history of the Wason selection task. In N. Galbraith (Ed.), *The thinking mind: A festschrift for Ken Manktelow* (pp. 1–14). Hove: Psychology Press.

Sloman, S. A., and Lagnado, D. (2015). Causality in thought. *Annual Review of Psychology, 66*, 223–47.

## Chapter 4: Decision making

LeBoeuf, R. A., and Shafir, E. (2005). Decision making. In K. Holyoak and R. G. Morrison (Eds), *The Cambridge handbook of thinking and reasoning* (pp. 243–65). Cambridge: Cambridge University Press.

Manktelow, K. I. (2012). *Thinking and reasoning: An introduction to the psychology of reason, judgement and decision making.* Hove: Psychology Press.

Newell, B., Lagnado, D. A. and Shanks, D. R. (2015). *Straight choices: The psychology of decision making* (2nd edition). Hove: Psychology Press.

## Chapter 5: Reasoning

Evans, J. St B. T. (2007). *Hypothetical thinking: Dual processes in reasoning and judgement.* Hove: Psychology Press.

Johnson-Laird, P. N. (2006). *How we reason.* Oxford: Oxford University Press.

Manktelow, K. I. (2012*). Thinking and reasoning: An introduction to the psychology of reason, judgement and decision making.* Hove: Psychology Press.

## Chapter 6: Are we rational?

Evans, J. St B. T. (2013). Two minds rationality. *Thinking & Reasoning,
20*, 129–46.

Gigerenzer, G. (2007). *Gut feelings: The intelligence of the unconscious.*
London: Penguin.

Nickerson, R. S. (2007). *Aspects of rationality: Reflections on what it
means to be rational and whether we are.* New York: Psychology
Press.

Stanovich, K. E. (2009). *What intelligence tests miss: The psychology
of rational thought.* New Haven and London: Yale University Press.

## Chapter 7: From dual processes to two minds

Evans, J. St B. T. (2010). *Thinking twice: Two minds in one brain.*
Oxford: Oxford University Press.

Kahneman, D. (2011). *Thinking, fast and slow.* New York: Farrar,
Straus and Giroux.

Stanovich, K. E. (2004). *The robot's rebellion: Finding meaning in the
age of Darwin.* Chicago: University of Chicago Press.

Further reading

# Index

# ONLINE CATALOGUE
## A Very Short Introduction

Our online catalogue is designed to make it easy to find your ideal Very Short Introduction. View the entire collection by subject area, watch author videos, read sample chapters, and download reading guides.

# SOCIAL MEDIA
## Very Short Introduction

# Join our community

www.oup.com/vsi

- Join us online at the official Very Short Introductions **Facebook** page.
- Access the thoughts and musings of our authors with our online **blog**.
- Sign up for our monthly **e-newsletter** to receive information on all new titles publishing that month.
- Browse the full range of Very Short Introductions online.
- Read **extracts** from the Introductions for free.
- Visit our library of **Reading Guides**. These guides, written by our expert authors will help you to question again, why you think what you think.
- If you are a teacher or lecturer you can order inspection copies quickly and simply via our website.